THE MAKING OF LANCASTER:
PEOPLE, PLACES AND WAR, 1789–1815

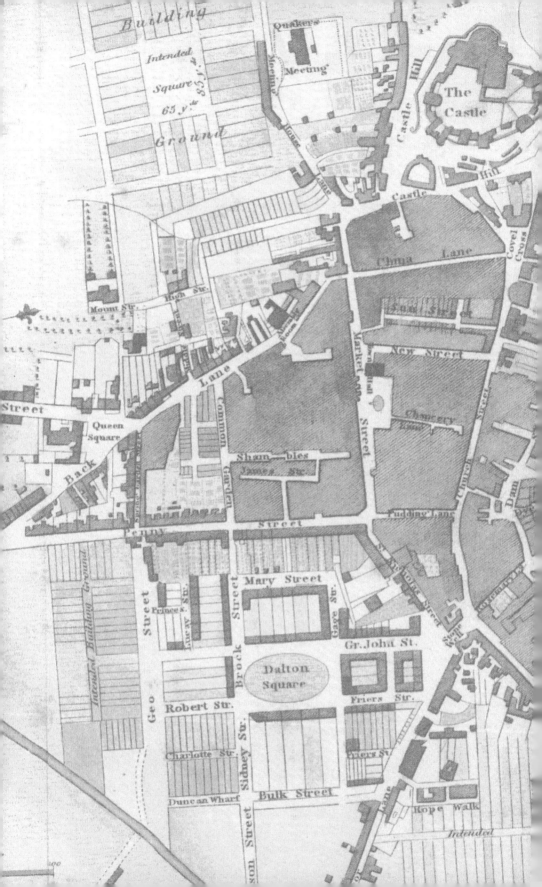

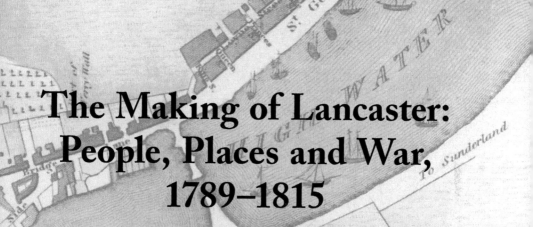

The Making of Lancaster:
People, Places and War,
1789–1815

G EORGE H OWSON

Copyright © George Howson, 2008, 2021

First edition published 2008, second edition 2021

Published by Palatine Books,
an imprint of Carnegie Publishing Ltd
Carnegie House,
Chatsworth Road,
Lancaster, LA1 4SL
www.carnegiepublishing.com

ISBN 978-1-910837-34-4

Typeset by Carnegie Book Production
Printed and bound by Totem

Contents

Acknowledgements

I would like to acknowledge with gratitude the help given throughout by the staff and former staff of the Lancaster City Reference Library (particularly Jenny Loveridge and Susan Wilson), the Lancaster Chamber of Commerce, the Lancashire Record Office in Preston, the National Archives at Kew and the British Library and the Guildhall Library in London. Also of great assistance have been the staff of Lancaster City Museum, The King's Own Royal Regimental Museum, Lancaster Maritime Museum, Liverpool Maritime Museum and the National Maritime Museum at Greenwich – all excellent places to visit. I would also like to thank the above for permission to use some of their pictures and maps and the Rev. Canon Peter Cavanagh, the Vicar of Lancaster, for permission to take photographs at the Priory Church of St Mary, Lancaster, and at St John's Church, Lancaster, and the Rev. Graham Pollitt for similar permission at Brookhouse Church. Many other individual persons have given their help, information and support, in particular John Champness, Judith Clarke, Jim Garbett, Emmeline Garnett, Ken Maunder, Dr Elizabeth Roberts, Peter Skidmore, Dr Andrew White, Dick White and Dr Michael Winstanley, all of Lancaster. From outside the area information has been received from David Milner and James Beckett, and from the descendants of Charles Gibson and William White. My gratitude is also due to Colin Burr and David Robbins the current trustees of the Greenwood Cup for allowing a photograph of the cup to be included. Absolutely invaluable has been Margaret Smith of Lonsdale Typesetting Services for the typing of my manuscript. Finally, thank you to everyone at Carnegie Publishing for bringing matters to a conclusion. If I have omitted any names I can only apologize.

For this second impression I would like to record my thanks to Ori Ben Chorin for permission to use the photographs of the cup presented to Capt Thomas Wilson. Also to Richard Poole for the picture of the unfortunate Hannah Smith. For general encouragement and support I would like to thank Melinda Elder and particularly Dr Michael Winstanley whose knowledge of both Lancaster and national history is enormous.

Lancaster
September 2020

Significant events, 1789–1820

1789   Outbreak of the French Revolution.

1793   Execution of King Louis XVI. Outbreak of war between England
         and France.

1794/95 First unsuccessful British campaign in the Netherlands.

1794   British naval victory over the French, 'The Glorious First of June'.

1794/96 Failed harvests and severe food shortages in Britain, together with
         food riots.

1797   Severe financial crisis. Bank of England suspends gold payments.
         Naval mutinies at Portsmouth and the Nore. Defeat of Spanish
         at Cape St Vincent and the Dutch at Camperdown. First French
         attempt to invade Ireland. Invasion fears in England.

1798   Rebellion in Ireland. French landings in Wales and Ireland. Defeat
         of French fleet at the Nile. French occupation of Egypt.

1799   Second unsuccessful British campaign in the Netherlands. Napoleon
         appointed First Consul of France.

1800   Further severe food shortages in Britain. Act of Union with Ireland.

1801   Danish fleet defeated at Copenhagen. French defeated in Egypt.
         Major invasion threat to southern England.

1802   Peace of Amiens between Britain and France. Most of British
         colonial conquests returned.

1803   In May war with France renewed. Major invasion fear 1803–1805
         from French army assembled at Boulogne.

1804   Napoleon becomes Emperor of the French.

1805   Defeat by French of Austrians and Russians at Ulm and Austerlitz.
         Defeat of French and Spanish fleet at Trafalgar.

1806–7   Further French victories against the Prussians and the Russians.
         Treaty of Tilsit (1807) between France and Russia loses Britain her
         last ally. Seizure of Danish fleet by Britain.

1806–11   Economic warfare between Britain, France and French-controlled Europe causes severe hardship in Britain.

1808   Outbreak of Peninsular War (Britain, Spain and Portugal against France with varying fortunes on either side).

1809   Unsuccessful British attack on Walcheren, Golden Jubilee of George III.

1809–10   Capture of Martinique, Guadalupe and Isle de France (Mauritius) completes destruction of French overseas empire.

1811   Prince of Wales (later George IV) takes over as Regent from George III, who is mentally incapacitated. Portugal cleared of the French. Capture of Dutch East Indies. Luddite riots begin.

1812   Luddite disturbances spread. Assassination of Spencer Percival (the Prime Minister). Military initiative in Spain passes to the allies. Napoleon invades Russia and reaches Moscow. Retreats from Moscow with catastrophic results. Outbreak of war between Britain and USA.

1813   Advance of Russian army across Germany, joined by Prussia, Austria and Sweden. Defeat of French at Leipzig. Spain cleared of the French. Economic conditions in Britain greatly improve.

1814   France invaded both from east and south-west. Paris falls in March and Napoleon abdicates in April and is exiled to Elba.

1815   War with USA ended. Corn Laws passed. Napoleon escapes from Elba and re-establishes himself in France ('The Hundred Days'). Heavily defeated by British and Prussians at Waterloo in June. Paris re-occupied by allies and Napoleon abdicates before being exiled permanently to St Helena.

1820   Death of George III.

To

Jane, Thomas and James Howson

Introduction

PRIOR TO THE OUTBREAK OF THE FIRST WORLD WAR IN 1914, the expression 'The Great War' referred to the war with France which lasted from 1793 to 1815. This struggle (with two short breaks measured in months rather than years) lasted from the famous French Revolution and fall of the Bourbon dynasty through into the next century and only ended on the bloodstained fields of Waterloo – a total of 23 years. Though the mainland of Britain largely escaped the passage of hostile armies with the attendant tale of shattered houses, ravaged crops, disease and death (Ireland is another story), it was nevertheless a war which for the first time involved most of society in one way or another. In a book published in 1828 a comment appeared:

> There are few families in the land who have not one or more relatives
> sleeping in a soldier's grave amongst the Spanish sierras and there is certainly
> not one who had not at some period or other during the contest a kinsman
> serving in the British ranks.[1]

The writer may be exaggerating slightly but in addition he should also have mentioned the tens of thousands of soldiers' graves in the fever swamps of the West Indies and India, in the deserts of Egypt, on the banks of the River Plate in Spanish America and the flat fields of the Low Countries. Fairness would also demand a reference to the thousands of seamen's graves in the Bay of Biscay, the Atlantic, the North Sea, the Baltic, the Indian Ocean or anywhere in the world where there was a sufficient depth of water for a ship-of-war to float. In fact, an examination of loss of life among servicemen indicates a proportionally higher rate of casualties than during the war of 1914–1918 – largely due to disease.

Lancaster itself was further away than many places in Britain from the scene of conflict but for various reasons, particularly because it was a port which reached the peak of its prosperity during the course of the war, could not remain untouched. Indeed, the degree to which Lancaster was affected

1

is perhaps the principal theme of this book. To those of us who still have memories of the Second World War when its six years seemed an eternity, the last and greatest conflict with France must have seemed like a lifetime, which for many people it was. A high proportion of the soldiers at Waterloo would have been born after the war had first begun and their fathers, grandfathers and great-grandfathers would have memories of the previous five struggles against the same enemy going back for more than the previous hundred years into the closing years of the seventeenth century. It may not perhaps be too much to wonder whether these conflicts still have an echo today and account for the hostility with which some in this country (and some sections of the press) still regard our neighbours across the Channel. If so, this is a pity because France is a truly great country whose past, present and doubtless its future place it in the front rank of the nations of the world.

Certainly, Lancaster at the end of the war in 1815 was a very different place than at the beginning. The rise of the West India trade was the whole basis of the steadily increasing prosperity of the town during the latter half

The old Public Bathhouse now a private house in Bath Street, off Moor Lane in Lancaster. It was erected by subscription and opened in 1803 at a cost of £500. The site was then in open fields outside the town.

PHOTOGRAPH: CARNEGIE

The Customs House on St George's Quay. It would have been a hive of activity during most of the period of the French Wars.

PHOTOGRAPH: CARNEGIE

of the eighteenth century. After a period of stagnation (though the trade was still considerable) its final collapse coincided with the end of the war. The reason for this will be explored in a later chapter but whatever those reasons were the physical and economic development of the town also slowed down and then largely stopped. As a consequence the place became something of a backwater for the next fifty years. Nevertheless, the period of prosperity can still be gauged by a walk round Lancaster, where the principal streets are still lined with Georgian buildings whose stone facades are still clearly visible above the shops and display windows of today. The same period was also responsible for many of the public buildings – churches, the Old Town Hall, Customs House, various alms houses, the Assembly Rooms, Skerton Bridge, plus of course most of the additions to the castle. Not all that existed still remains but enough does to give a flavour of the town as the late eighteenth century slipped into the early nineteenth – indeed a Georgian town cut off in its prime.

Other themes involve a close look at some of the individuals involved in the West India trade, their ships and their varying fortunes. The lives of some members of what were then called the higher ranks of society are examined in some detail and again as to how they were affected by the war – in some cases very seriously. In addition, insofar as surviving records permit, the rest of the electorate is looked at (quite large compared with many other places), the ordinary townspeople and what might be called the underclass who left few if any records behind them. One chapter is devoted to the lives of female Lancastrians and again lack of records prevents any study in depth, society being at that time a very male-oriented conception.

The war period also coincided with the first part of that change in the make-up of the country known as the 'industrial revolution'. This fundamental development, coupled with the physical and economic consequences of the war, placed unparalleled strain on the social fabric of the country – perhaps the most severe the nation has ever experienced. Although Lancaster avoided the worst effects of these changes it could not escape them entirely. Again, it is hoped that this involvement, albeit peripheral, will appear in subsequent pages.

Nevertheless, it is clear that all the people mentioned above, together with their anonymous fellow citizens, were in one way or another actors on the local stage and were to a greater or lesser extent the men and women who directly or indirectly played their part in some of the most tumultuous, terrifying and important years of British history. Hopefully, present-day Lancastrians will find their lives and experiences of interest.

CHAPTER ONE

Setting the Scene

I N 1793 Lancaster was a market town dominated physically by the ancient castle and St Mary's parish church – now known as Lancaster Priory. The castle, as county gaol and venue of the twice yearly assizes was in the early stages of its renovation and enlargement to its present-day appearance. The town itself was quite small in area, bounded by the castle, the quay, King Street, Queen Street, the newly laid out Dalton Square and St Leonardsgate. The soon-to-be-built canal opened in 1797 ran through open countryside and only touched the town at the top of Penny Street.

In 1784 Lancaster's population (excluding seamen) was 8584, rising slowly to 9030 in 1801 and 9247 in 1811. The latter figures are those from the first two official censuses. The figures are for the parish of Lancaster only and do not include parts of present-day Lancaster such as Skerton, Scotforth, Bulk or Aldcliffe.[1] The first two censuses contain nothing like the information available from a census of the late nineteenth and early twentieth century but it would appear that most people in 1801 were employed in trade, with very many fewer employed in agriculture. Ten years later the effect of the economic trade war with France can be seen, with fewer people in employment of any kind and a substantial rise in those not in work.

For the same reason the physical expansion of the town slowed down or even stopped. Clark's map of Lancaster dated 1807 (featured in this book) optimistically showed a number of residential streets which were in fact never built – on the riverside site adjacent to the recently built Skerton Bridge and the area almost opposite the Friends' Meeting House now occupied by Dallas Road and Blades Street. Only Dalton Square today shows what might have been had the various plans come to fruition. At all events a study of the three relevant street plans, Mackareth 1778, Clark and finally Binns 1821, shows a fascinating picture of the gradual development of the town. Any further extension was probably prevented by the double bank failure in the 1820s mentioned later as well as the recession at the end of the war in 1815.

Notwithstanding the many examples of Georgian architecture mentioned in the Introduction, and which of course still remain, and the number which have for one reason or another been demolished, Lancaster would not, to modern eyes at least, present a wholly pleasing appearance. The bulk of the residential property would be stone-built with stone-flagged or slated roofs. Some thatched cottages still existed. However, the streets were dark, badly lit and narrow. There was no running water and the sewage arrangements were primitive. The sights and stenches must have been appalling, particularly in the less affluent parts of the town and in the Shambles where animals were slaughtered for sale in the adjoining butchers' shops. Much of the raw sewage ended up in the Dalton Dam, being the old watercourse (which still exists under the present-day street system) which ran through the lower part of the town roughly on the line of the present-day North Road and Damside Street before emptying itself into the River Lune. A thrice yearly cattle market was held, when hundreds and sometimes thousands of beasts were driven on the hoof through the streets – with entirely predictable results as to hygiene. In May 1795 the diarist David Cragg noted:

> At the fair at this time, the Cattle stood in the Church Street,
> Pudding Lane and Penny Street, in the Broadway [?], pretty thick
> to the bottom, and at the Stone Well and a considerable way on
> Leonardsgate and up into Moor Lane.[2]

and on November 1805, the *Lancaster Gazette* reported that nearly 3000 head of cattle passed through Lancaster *en route* to Garstang Fair. Doubtless such matters would be regarded as an everyday fact of life.

The largest individual employers throughout the period were probably the two local shipyards: Brockbanks on the south side of the river, roughly on the site now occupied by Sainsbury's supermarket; and Smiths on the other side of the river, near to the end of the Millennium Bridge, probably a little downstream from the site of Our Lady's High School. Both the shipyards and the extensive shipping activity of the late eighteenth and early nineteenth centuries were of course complementary to each other and mutually self-supporting.[3] It seems that approximately one hundred ships were built in Lancaster between 1790 and 1820, though it is not possible to be entirely accurate. Of that total, perhaps about half were intended for and took part in the West India trade, though not all traded from Lancaster itself. This emphasis on shipbuilding also supported many other allied industries, such as sail-cloth making, sail-making itself, rope-making and an anchor-smith. Other manufacturing processes partly connected with the West India trade

General view of Lancaster with a ship under construction at Brockbank's shipyard.
Painted in the early nineteenth century by Gideon Yates.

© LANCASTER CITY MUSEUM, PART OF LANCASHIRE MUSEUMS

were the making of candles, soap, sugar-refining and furniture-making, which
at this time was not just restricted to the well-known firm of Gillows – the
Gillow family itself appearing to have severed its active involvement in the
business sometime between 1811 and 1814.

Despite its location in out-of-the-way north-west England, Lancaster kept
well in touch with other parts of England and Scotland. There were excellent
coaching services (which improved during the period covered by this book),
some in private hands, others provided by the Royal Mail coaches which
carried passengers as well as mail, parcels and newspapers to and from London
and other major towns such as Manchester and Liverpool. They were expensive
and humbler citizens either walked or travelled on goods wagons which ran
scheduled services like the coaches but at a very much slower pace.

CANDLE-HOUSE, &c.
TO BE LET,

And entered upon at May-Day next,

A Good CANDLE-HOUSE, situated in St. Leonard-gate, Lancaster, with a ROOM over it; and also a good CELLAR, in the possession of Mr. Henry Postlethwaite, as tenant.

For further particulars apply to Mr. RICHARD WALLER, of Haverbrack, near Millthorp, the owner; or Mr. JOHN HODGSON, cabinet-maker, in Moor-lane, Lancaster, who will shew the premises.

N. B. The above is well adapted for the liquor business, or a joiner's shop.

Candles were one of the principal local exports to the West Indies.

WITH KIND PERMISSION OF LANCASHIRE LIBRARIES

The coaches, both private and Royal Mail, would use the bigger inns in the town as their calling points – the 'old' King's Arms, the Sun, the Royal Oak and the Commercial Inn, the latter two situated in Market Square but both now demolished well over a hundred years ago. Some passenger traffic also took place on the canal which if the passenger was not in a hurry was probably the most comfortable way of getting to Preston – though the journey did in the early days at least take several hours.

Writing in 1807, Clark also mentions two breweries (after 1802), tobacco, snuff and pipe makers, and finally the several hat manufacturers. There was one solitary cotton-spinning mill. There were also two banks. It is clear that many of these manufacturers, together with the handloom weavers, operated on a small scale and were more in the nature of cottage industries. Nevertheless, membership of the local benefit or friendly societies, who must have recruited largely from these activities, remained reasonably constant at about 2000 until the end of the Napoleonic wars, when they declined.[4] However, in a labour-intensive age, employment was very diverse and clearly a lot of people of both sexes worked in domestic service, in shops, in the public houses and the inns of the town, or as miscellaneous labourers. Obviously, in the Lune Valley and other rural parts – that came right up to the edge of the town – many of them were either farmers or agricultural labourers, though many of the villages did have their own individual manufacturers providing employment. Nevertheless, all were involved in the life of Lancaster, which they used (as both the buyers and the sellers) as a market town in the correct sense of the word at the Wednesday and Saturday markets. All those in

NEVER-FAILING CURE FOR THE
I T C H,
IN TWENTY-FOUR HOURS.

TO those afflicted with the above disorder, BARCLAY'S ORIGINAL OINTMENT is recommended as a *safe, speedy,* and *effectual* remedy. . This Ointment has been in general use for upwards of seventy years, without a single instance of its having failed to cure the most inveterate cases. It does not contain the smallest particle of mercury, or any other dangerous ingredient, and may be safely used by persons of the most delicate constitution. The public are requested to observe, that none can possibly be *genuine,* unless signed by the proprietors, BARCLAY and SON, and great danger may arise from the neglect of this caution.

Sold, wholesale and retail, by Barclay and Son, (the *only* successors to Jackson and Co.) No. 95, Fleet-market, London, price 1s. 9d. duty included; and, by their appointment, by W. Minshull, Printer of this Paper, Walmsley, and Turner, Lancaster; Bell, Garstang; Walker, Croft, and Addison, Preston; Schofield, and Hartley, Rochdale; Branthwaite, Kendal; Jollie, Carlisle; Soulby, Penrith; Bannister, Blackburn; Simcock, Wigan; Gardner, Bolton; Soulby, Ulverston; Foster, Kirkby Lonsdale; and every medicine vender in the kingdom.

The Itch was clearly a major problem – probably due to a mixture of poor diet and lack of proper washing facilities. The local paper carried this advertisement for years.

employment worked by today's standards very long hours and as a consequence of this and the existing level of wages the scope for leisure activities and relaxation would be strictly limited. For those not in the wage-earning ranks, the opportunities were greater: with the Amicable Lending Library, the Assembly Rooms, the News Rooms, the two Masonic Lodges, the Musical and Agricultural Societies. All social classes would, however, meet in apparent harmony, if not in equality, at the theatre, at church, at the racecourse and

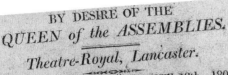

Playbills from the Lancaster Theatre, then as now in St Leonardgate. The principal seasons were usually in March/April and August/September to coincide with the twice-yearly Assizes. These, together, with the balls and other social functions held in the (still existing) Assembly Rooms in King Street attracted the county gentry of Westmorland and North Lancashire.

WITH KIND PERMISSION OF LANCASHIRE LIBRARIES

BY DESIRE OF THE
QUEEN of the ASSEMBLIES.

Theatre-Royal, Lancaster.

This present FRIDAY, AUGUST 18th, 1809,

The Favourite COMEDY of

Wives as they Were,

AND

Maids as they Are.

Sir William Dorillon,   Mr. SHARPLEY.
Lord Priory,   Mr. YATES.
Sir George Evelyn,   Mr. MORELAND.
Mr. Bronzley,   Mr. COWAN.
Mr. Norberty,   Mr. HEMLEY.
Nabson,   Mr. PRIOR.
Oliver,   Mr. P?LEY.
Miss Dorillon,   Mrs.
Lady Mary Raffle,   Mrs.
Lady Priory,   Mrs.

END OF THE PLAY,

Two favourite SONGS, by M

To conclude with the favourite Farc

High Life belou

Lovel,
Freeman,
Lord Duke's Servant,
Sir Harry's Servant,
Phillip,
Tom,
Coachman,
Mrs. Kitty, (with a Song,)
Lady Bab's Maid,
Lady Charlotte's Maid,
Cook,
Chloe,

Lower Boxes 3s.—Upper Boxes 2s. 6d.—Pit 2s.—Gallery
begin precisely at seven o'C

Tickets to be had of Mr. STANTON, at Mr. Marmaduke Ba
Printer, New-Street, Lancaster, where Places

Mr. Incledon

Having arrived in Lancaster on Monday Evening, he will Perform this present Tuesday, being positively the ONLY NIGHT he can appear in Lancaster this Season, having to perform in Shrewsbury on Wednesday.

THEATRE, LANCASTER.

On TUESDAY, September 3d, 1799,

The favourite PLAY of The

BEGGARS OPERA

Capt. Macheath,   Mr. INCLEDON

Peachum,   Mr. DAWSON
Lockit,   Mr. SEYMOUR
Filch,   Mr. CRISP
Mat o' the Mint, Mr. HAYES
Ben Budge,   Mr. HARGRAVE
Drawer,   Mr. MAYCOCK
Polly,   Mrs. COOKE
Lucy Lockit,   Mrs. CRISP
Jenny Diver, Mrs. DAWSON——Mrs Peachum,   Mrs. HARGRAVE

In the Course of the Evening, the favourite Hunting SONG of

OLD TOWLER,

GAY'S ADMIRED BALLAD OF

BLACK EY'D SUSAN,

And GEORGE ALEXANDER STEEVEN's celebrated

DESCRIPTION of a STORM,

BY

Mr. INCLEDON.

With the MUSICAL FARCE of

LOCK and KEY.

Cheerly,   Mr. DAWSON
Brumagem,   Captain Vane,
Mr. ASKER——Page, Mr. HARGRAVE
Ralph,   Mr. MAYCOCK
                  Mr. CRISP
Fanny,   Mrs. CRISP——Dolly,   Mrs. HARGRAVE
Laura,   Mrs. COOKE

the electoral hustings, although the latter were not always peaceful. The most popular events for spectators were undoubtedly the twice-yearly public (and frequently multiple) hangings – before 1800 at the top of Wyresdale Road and after that date behind the castle. These were followed in popularity by whippings or exposure in the pillory in the Market Square, the chairing of the victorious election candidates, the annual parade of the friendly societies, and during the war years the continuous movement of military units, preferably with a band, throughout the district.

The town government of the time was in the hands of the Mayor and Corporation, the latter consisting of a Recorder, seven Aldermen, two Bailiffs, twelve Capital Burgesses and twelve Common Councilmen. There was no nonsense about democracy: the Corporation continued on a self-electing and self-perpetuating basis, drawing its membership from the local freemen. The bulk of the Corporation's income appears to have come from rents on property owned by the Corporation and tolls levied on people using the market as well as the fees paid by those becoming freemen. The Corporation was restricted by law to members of the established Church of England. This precluded both Protestant dissenters and Roman Catholics from the responsibilities and perquisites of local government, but not from other bodies such as the Port Commissioners, numerous charities, and business and commercial affairs, where the Quakers in particular were active and influential beyond their numbers.

However, Lancaster seems to have been a tolerant place. Both Roman Catholics (including the highly respected Dr Rigby, the priest who officiated at the new chapel in Dalton Square) and Protestant dissenters were members of the somewhat elitist Merchants' Newsroom in Market Street. On the whole, too, charitable giving was quite generous, evidenced by the alms houses for both men and women, the Dispensary on Castle Hill where medical assistance on an out-patient basis was administered free of charge. Finally, large sums were donated to the needy in times of economic hardship and of course special collections were made for the wounded and bereaved after the victories at Trafalgar and Waterloo.

In 1794 the Universal British Directory published a directory for just about every town in the country – Lancaster included. Prior to listing the names and addresses of the principal inhabitants and the various trades and shops in the town it gives quite a lengthy preamble giving something of the history of the place. Of much greater interest is the information supplied on current affairs in Lancaster. Referring to the political make-up it says:

View of Skerton Bridge erected 1788 by the County Council and designed by Thomas Harrison. The painting is early nineteenth century and is by Gideon Yates.

© LANCASTER CITY MUSEUM PART OF LANCASHIRE MUSEUMS

By the charter freemen only have the vote but the most glaring corruption lies in making those freemen. A freeman's son or freeman's apprentice within the borough is entitled to take up his freedom whenever he pleases on paying into the hand of the mayor... the sum of £1-7-6 [£1.37]. This sum is most generally paid by the opposing candidates and the greatest number of freemen thus made turns the scale of the election. As ship-building and the cabinet business are the only manufacturers there [not correct], he who has the most ships to build or repair or he who will lay out a few hundreds of pounds in mahogany furniture, is most likely to carry his election. The journeymen are at the command of their masters; they get intoxicated during the canvass and having 5s [25p] to eat and drink on the day of the election, they give a shout and go quietly to work again.

Following this somewhat cynical but not wholly inaccurate account of an election campaign the writer goes on:

> The town is much enlarged, the new houses are particularly neat and handsome, the streets are well paved and thronged with inhabitants busied in a prosperous trade to Guinea and the West Indies; a long fine quay and noble warehouses built and when it shall please those concerned to deepen the shoals in the river ships of a greater burden may lie before them.

Alas this work was never done and the results are visible today. However, the writer continues: 'The air of Lancaster is salubrious, the environs pleasant and the inhabitants wealthy, courteous, hospitable and polite.' It all sounds a little too good to be true. Nevertheless, this was Lancaster or something like it when the French Revolution broke out in July 1789 and things were never quite the same again.

The Powder House in Powderhouse Lane, Torrisholme, Lancaster. Ships anchored at the quay were obliged to store their gunpowder in the building for safety reasons during their stay in the port.

PHOTOGRAPH: CARNEGIE

CHAPTER TWO

The other half

O F NECESSITY most of the people who appear in the following pages are men. In accordance with the times in which they lived men were entirely dominant throughout most of society. Everybody in the army and navy (not surprisingly) was male, as were the members of the professions such as medicine, law and the Church. To a large extent so were trade and commerce. In Lancaster the freemen (who alone had the vote), membership of the town council and the Merchants' Coffee Room was also entirely a male preserve. Interestingly the Amicable Lending Library had both men and many women as members, and of course both sexes attended church, the theatre and probably the races. The historical records about women are slight: they left few documents themselves, while other people only seldom made meaningful references to them: therefore, just over one half of the local population was all but invisible except in the births, marriages and deaths column of the local paper.

The better-off women, if married, would spend their time bringing up their children and managing their households which, together with their leisure time, could be done supported by a number of servants, both male and female. They might well involve themselves in church matters and charitable work – particularly if they were associated with the evangelical St Ann's church in Moor Lane and the Quaker meeting then, as now, in Meeting House Lane. However, those in humbler circumstances and the unmarried had to earn a living either in employment or as self-employed. There were two directories for Lancaster, published in 1794 and 1811 respectively, although the earlier is a much more comprehensive work. This lists some twenty-one self-employed women, almost all running their own shops. This was roughly ten per cent of the total. They included Mary Brockbank, the widowed sister-in-law of the shipbuilder, who was a sail-maker. In the admittedly less satisfactory 1811 directory the figures were substantially lower – twelve persons, approximately four per cent of the total. Andrew White in his *History of Lancaster*[1] draws attention to the Noon family of whom

VERY SUPERIOR TRAVELLING.
The public are most respectfully informed,
THAT A NEW AND ELEGANT
LIGHT POST-COACH,
CALLED
THE ROYAL PILOT,
Carrying only Four Insides, commenced running
from the King's-Arms and Royal-Oak Inns,
Lancaster,
On Wednesday the 16th day of November,
At eleven o'clock in the forenoon,
TO PRESTON AND LIVERPOOL,
Where it arrives at seven o'clock in the evening,
and will continue to run every WEDNESDAY,
FRIDAY, and SUNDAY.
The above Coach will return from Liverpool every
TUESDAY, THURSDAY, and SATURDAY, and will
arrive at Lancaster at half-past two o'clock in
the afternoon, will proceed to Kendal, at three,
the same days.
THE TELEGRAPH COACH,
For Preston, Liverpool, Manchester, London,
and all parts in the South, every morning, at eight
o'clock, as usual; also to Kendal, Penrith, Carlisle,
Whitehaven, and all parts of Scotland, every even-
ing, at six o'clock.   JON. DUNN and CO.
GENERAL COACH-OFFICE, MARKET-
STREET, CORNER OF SUN-STREET.

There were regular coach services from Lancaster to Preston, Liverpool, Manchester
and London and of course across the sands to the Furness area of Lancashire.
The Dunn family later built the house in Ryelands Park subsequently occupied by
Lord Ashton until his death in 1931.

WITH KIND PERMISSION OF LANCASHIRE LIBRARIES

three generations of women ran the Royal Oak Hotel in Market Square
– where the public library now stands. This was one of the principal such
establishments in Lancaster, alongside the King's Arms at the top of Market
Street and the Commercial Inn also in Market Square. These provided
stage coach and mail coach departure points, accommodation for travellers,
venues for formal dinners and eating facilities for the townspeople and those
attending the weekly markets. The last of the three was Jane Noon, who
was the licensee of the Royal Oak from the death of her mother in 1803 to
the mid-1830s. Jane Noon had a younger sister, Elizabeth, who had a straw
hat business but in addition was for many years the town's postmistress. She
succeeded to that responsible position on the death of her father, Thomas
Noon, who before being postmaster had been a tallow chandler. Elizabeth

Shortage of small change at the end of the eighteenth century led to many local traders
all over the country to issue their own token currency. Lancaster was no exception as
these illustrations show. Those issuing them were obliged to exchange them for coins of
the realm on request. The smaller of the coins were issued by Daniel Eccleston of
Lancaster in 1794.

PHOTOGRAPHS: CARNEGIE

Noon seems to have been the channel for the London newspapers (probably delivered by mail coach) and certainly sold them to the Merchants' News Room and doubtless to others as well. Together with all the above, she was also local agent for the British Insurance Company.[2] Both sisters must have been well known to almost everyone in Lancaster and quite formidable people in their own right.

A notable example of self-help in Lancaster throughout our period was the Friendly Society – there being separate ones for both men and women. Trade unions, or combinations as they were then called, were mainly forbidden, but friendly societies were actively encouraged by Act of Parliament – doubtless partly to encourage thrift and partly to make an application for poor law relief less likely. Each year on Whit Monday both the male and female societies assembled in Dalton Square before proceeding, headed by a band, to the parish church for a service. Afterwards all the members adjourned to the various public houses which formed their headquarters and meeting places for a dinner where they spent the rest of the day in 'conviviality and harmony'. In 1805 there were fourteen male societies and three female. The former had a membership varying between 361 (The Samaritans) to 66 (The Provident). The female societies had 80, 69 and 56 members, respectively. Each member made a small weekly contribution and relief would be paid when members were sick or would defray the cost of the funeral when a member had died. Male membership fluctuated around the 2,000 mark during the war and female about 200 or slightly fewer. This must represent a vey high proportion not only of the working population but the population as a whole. Though perhaps the figures include people living just outside the town. A decline set in after the end of the war, doubtless reflecting the recession. It is interesting that there were so many women in Lancaster who had the initiative and the confidence to form and then to run these societies. In 1795 the president of the Female Amicable Society was Ann Hoole but the treasurer was a man – John Smith, a schoolmaster. In 1810 the president of the Female Benevolent Society, which met at the Bull's Head in Pudding Lane (now Cheapside), was a Betty Berry and the two stewards Sarah Hall and Margaret Monsey. Like their successors the following year, Millison (*sic*) Anderton, Mary Harrison and Esther Leatherbarrow, none of them could write and they were compelled to sign documents with their mark only.[3] Although these societies were in part social and the weekly subscriptions were used in part to pay for drink, they must have played a vital part in relieving some of the effects of illness and death, together with the satisfaction gained from communal effort, association and fellowship.[4]

PARDON ASKED.

WHEREAS we, the undersigned ROBERT BATTERSBY and JAMES FOSTER, both of Quarmore, in the county of Lancaster, labourers, did, on the evening of Sunday the tenth day of September instant, at Halton, in the said county, violently assault and abuse THOMAS ESCOLME, constable of Halton aforesaid, whilst in the execution of his office, he the said Thomas Escolme being sent for to quell a disturbance, raised by us, in the dwelling-house of Jacob Martin, of Halton aforesaid, innkeeper :— And whereas the said Thomas Escolme hath actually commenced a prosecution against us for the said assault ; but, in consideration of our asking this public pardon, and of paying the expence already incurred, and the expence of inserting this advertisement in The Lancaster Gazette, the said Thomas Escolme hath consented that no further proceedings shall be had against us, Now we, the said Robert Battersby and James Foster, do hereby ask pardon of the said Thomas Escolme for the said offence.—Dated this 25th day of September, 1809.

The mark
ROBERT ✗ BATTERSBY.
of
The mark
JAMES ✗ FOSTER,
of
Witness : Thos. Thomson

A sensible way of sorting out a dispute in a Halton public house in 1809. Notice the spelling for 'Quarmore' reflecting the local pronunciation.

Perhaps the only paid occupation open to women of a higher social status and education would be that of a governess or schoolmistress and there are references to both in the local press – such as, for example, Miss Shaw, who advertised her school on Castle Hill in July 1809.

Some further evidence of women at the other end of the social scale can also be found in certain of the surviving legal records. One such example is a complaint from a Mary Cooper who in May 1808 alleged that one Betty

McCree had struck her violently in the face and called her 'a damn'd whore and made use of very lewd and threatening language'.[5] Unfortunately, apart from the fact that both women were married to sailors, nothing more is known of this incident. Inevitably, as in most towns and cities (particularly perhaps seaports with a transient male population), there were a number of women who, presumably for payment, would supply more personal services to men. One such was Elizabeth Swainson, who was brought before the quarter sessions at Lancaster Castle in 1802 charged with running a disorderly house (a polite word for a brothel) in Skerton. Her husband was also a seaman ('at sea'). She pleaded guilty and was sentenced to six months' imprisonment in the House of Correction in Preston.[6] She was luckier than Jane Harper who in July 1811 received a sentence of two years, also for running a disorderly house, this time on the Quay.[7] Generally speaking, however, Lancaster seems to have been a law-abiding town. Most of the people dealt with at the assizes for the more serious offences came from other parts of the county and the matters dealt with at the borough sessions were fairly trivial, such as giving short measure to drinkers in a public house, having inaccurate weighing scales in shops, leaving rubbish in the streets and allowing animals, particularly pigs and fierce dogs, to roam the streets.

If women of the late eighteenth and early nineteenth centuries remain fairly invisible to modern researchers, so do their children, usually appearing only when they die – frequently from accidents such as drowning, falling from a height, being burned in the home or falling under the wheels of a passing wagon or even after being struck on the head by the sails of a windmill.[8] Many, of course, died even younger of some childhood disease or in childbirth along with their unfortunate mother.

The contemporary press often gave accounts of dinners (always male) held to celebrate some civic occasion or national celebration and from time to time would list the toasts given after the meal. Frequently one of these toasts was to 'The Lancashire Witches', i.e. the ladies. This was always greeted with great applause and sometimes with three cheers. The wives must have been glad to know that they had not been entirely forgotten.[9]

CHAPTER THREE

The parson and the farmer

B RYAN WALLER was born in Church Street, Lancaster, in 1765, although the family seem to have had connections with Ingleton. His father was a tallow chandler. He attended the Lancaster grammar school and subsequently Trinity College, Cambridge, graduating in 1788. He appears to have been quite well connected, being related to the Wilsons of Dallam Tower and to Richard Watson, the bishop of Llandaff. He had a brother, Will, who was a sugar planter and slave owner or manager in Jamaica and who died unmarried in 1804. A rough diary kept by Bryan Waller (or at least a copy) has survived, which gives some indication of his life in Lancaster and London and his thoughts particularly during the last years of the eighteenth century.[1] He was a freeman of Lancaster, which conferred upon him the right to vote, and he would travel by coach between Cambridge and Lancaster for that purpose. Living in London, he would walk long distances around the capital; he would visit the theatre, and saw the well-known contemporary actors Mrs Siddons and John Phillip Kemble perform; he even went to Newgate prison to see the deranged Lord George Gordon. He appears to have had sufficient money to lead a life of some leisure while in London; he had many friends and acquaintances there, with whom he often supped on 'toasted cheese and porter'. Being a graduate member of Cambridge University, he had a second vote for the university Member of Parliament and he would receive circular letters from the then MP William Pitt, seeking his support – which was gladly given. He was also sufficiently open minded to attend Quaker meetings and a Catholic mass. He also wrote quite a lot of poetry, some of which was published. To present-day eyes it seems of a fairly forgettable nature. Bryan Waller was something of a social climber and relished his contacts with the aristocracy. For a while he was tutor to Lord Pollington, the son of the earl of Mexborough, and earned the sum of fifty guineas thereby.

Among the poems he had written he had sent some to Edmund Burke, the renowned politician, writer and thinker. A meeting between Waller and Burke then followed and between April and June 1792 they were in regular contact.

The Rev. Bryan Waller 1765–1841, a native of
Lancaster, and later for many years vicar of
Burton in Kendal.

For a time Waller acted as a kind
of personal secretary to Burke,
translating and writing for him.
Burke is perhaps best known for
his work *Reflections on the French
Revolution*, published two years
previously, which was hostile to the
events in France, and Waller clearly
shared those views. His diary indicates
his lack of sympathy to the progress of the
revolution in France.

In the summer of 1792 he returned to Lancaster and in November he recorded
drinking tea and spending an evening on board a vessel tied up at Lancaster
quayside. On 10 August 1792 he recorded 'dreadful and ferocious insurrection in
Paris'. On 9 January, 1793 Waller wrote: 'The first turf for the canal from Kendal
to West Houghton was cut this day.' Two weeks later he recorded: 'News arrived
that the usurpers in France had passed sentence of death upon his most Christian
Majesty Louis 16th on Tuesday, the 17th instant. The gloom that pervaded the
breasts of Englishmen on this occasion is better conceived than described –
sorrow mingled with indignation.' Three days later on the 26th Waller's diary
notes: 'Intelligence in the newspapers that the king of France was beheaded on
Monday, the 21st instant at twenty-two minutes past 10 a.m.'

He was ordained a clergyman in the Church of England in 1795 and spent
the next few years trying to obtain a comfortable living, preferably in the
south of England within travelling distance of London. His correspondence
shows that he clearly longed for the literary and social life of the metropolis,
but was not successful.[2] He did, however, officiate at many church services,
both in London and the Lancaster district. His diary tailed off after the turn
of the century, with only brief entries thereafter, but finally he was appointed
vicar of Burton in Kendal in 1806, a position he retained until his death in
1842 at the age of 78. He married very late in life and fathered two children
when he was in his seventies. Interestingly his granddaughter Eleonor died

at Milnthorpe as recently as 1954, at the age of 80.[3] There cannot have been many people alive in that year whose grandfather remembered the death of Louis XVI and whose great-uncle managed a slave plantation.

A very different man was David Cragg of Ortner in Wyresdale, a member of a family long settled in that area. He was a farmer, as was his father, and both were or became members of the Society of Friends and clearly not part of the Establishment. Like other members of the family, David Cragg left a diary, or journal, which records in some detail events in and around Lancaster and Wyresdale, particularly in the 1790s.[4] Cragg was clearly an eye-witness of many of these events, and he gives a vivid picture not only of purely family matters but also of a series of riotous incidents, bad weather, crimes committed, suicides and the follies of his neighbours, particularly John Fenton Cawthorne of Wyreside Hall, for whom he entertained an intense dislike. Of all these more later.

Cragg was clearly well aware of the happenings in France and took a radically different view of things than Bryan Waller. In 1791 he writes critically of the riots in Birmingham when dissenting meeting-houses and the houses of dissenters (including that of the well-known scientist Dr Priestley) were wrecked by a loyalist mob. The following year (1792) he notes:

> Glorious successes of the French army against the despot and slaves and tyrants which they are fighting with ... see, ye tyrants, the progress of liberty and tremble at your merited fate.

Shortly afterwards Cragg noted that the British government made several proclamations 'against Libel and Seditious Books said to be in circulation and I suppose *The Rights of Man* by Thomas Paine is one of the principal books against them'. The diarist's language becomes more strident, with references to 'that useless, extravagant king or despot of ours'; and when the Militia was called out: 'two men of war, five frigates put into commission, so that there is hope for a revolution in England. I for myself hope so ... England will rise the day it falls out with France.'

Cragg quite understandingly has numerous grievances, in particular the system of impressment for the navy, the game laws, tithes, and tolls, and produces cogent arguments against them all.

Like Bryan Waller he is aware of the rapidly moving events in France: 'The French are trying the king for treason and very likely he will be beheaded erelong. I pity the poor king, I think they should not put him to death. I

Parental consent for the marriage of diarist David Cragg.

FRL 2/1/11/158. REPRODUCED BY PERMISSION OF THE COUNTY ARCHIVIST,
LANCASHIRE RECORD OFFICE

would let him live but there is no chance of that scarcely at all.' And finally on 28 January: 'The king of France was executed last Monday at noon, so that is an end to him.'

There is no indication as to where Cragg obtained his information. He is clearly highly literate and his journal gives impressive details of his reading. He is well informed and familiar with the identities of the leaders of the Whig party – Charles James Fox, Grey and others – and indicates his strong support for their policies. He must have had fairly regular access to a newspaper but to which one is not clear. Newspapers at this date were published in Liverpool, Manchester and Whitehaven – the first Lancaster paper did not appear until 1801. However, some of the more affluent members of the Quaker community in Lancaster were members of the Merchants' Coffee-room in Market Street where London newspapers were available and it is known that these were passed or sold on to non-members.

It is not known to what extent Cragg's political views were shared by others and if so how many – certainly not by Bryan Waller. However, one may be sure he was not alone in his thoughts. In many parts of the country there were like-minded people, members of what were known as corresponding societies, particularly the London Corresponding Society, which openly gave support to the new regime in France. However, their influence diminished following the violent excesses in Paris and elsewhere. France had been at war with Austria and Prussia since the summer of 1792 and throughout the autumn of that year relations between Britain and France deteriorated sharply. Both sides took steps which increased the tension between the two countries and by the end of the year conflict seemed almost inevitable. The execution of the French king of itself almost precipitated an immediate break with France, but the latter put the matter beyond doubt with a formal declaration of war against Britain on 1 February 1793. Cragg's reactions showed his despair:

> Now sounds the dreadful trumpet of war. There will be nothing but fire and sword, desolation and fighting, up to the knees in blood. All Europe has taken the alarm and are determined to crush the poor French because they have thrown off the yoke of servitude … I hope the French will not only be able to obtain all their liberty but to give all those who fight against them a most hearty drubbing.

Such sentiments would clearly put the diarist at odds with most of his fellow countrymen. Initially a new war against the French, both regicides and republicans, was not too unpopular and government in London would soon take steps against those in society it felt could not be trusted. Cragg clearly realised the danger he was putting himself in when he wrote:

> I will say no more. My father has commanded me to write nothing about the war or Thomas Paine or politics of any sort, for if anybody saw what I have already written I should be tried for libel and perhaps hanged. If any disturbance should take place I should be first to burn this book, which would grieve me ill.

He was not alone in being careful. The Lancaster Amicable Library was a lending library with subscribers among the commercial, professional and leisured citizens of Lancaster. Among the books listed in their catalogue were both Burke's *Reflections on the Revolution in France* and Paine's *The Rights of Man*. A minute of the Library Committee, dated 24 July 1793, states bluntly: 'It is ordered that Paine's *The Rights of Man* should be locked up and expunged from the catalogue and prevented for circulation.'[5]

By now hostilities had commenced on land and sea, and quite soon the war would touch the lives of all the inhabitants of Lancaster. David Cragg subsequently emigrated to Canada with much of his family and died there in 1835. His descendants live there today. We shall return to Cragg later in this book.

· CHAPTER FOUR ·

Seamen in Lancaster

A T THE BEGINNING of the 1790s Lancaster was at the height of its golden age as a port. Despite severe shipping losses to both French and rebel American privateers during the War of American Independence, which ended in 1783, the overseas trade of the town was thriving. Wartime losses were made good and both of Lancaster's shipbuilding concerns were kept busy, producing about forty seagoing ships, averaging about 200 tons, between 1790 and 1799. It is perhaps the West Indian trade in which Lancaster was so much involved which has held the attention both of local historians and local tradition. Certainly for a small town with navigational problems both for the river and for Glasson Dock the passage of ships to and from the West Indies islands was remarkable, with forty-seven ships making the crossing in 1790, rising to fifty-seven nine years later. This turned out to be the peak year. Thereafter a decline set in, but nevertheless the trade did continue through to the end of the war in 1815.[1]

Tradition has also focused on the slave or 'African' trade. During the 1760s this trade had been extensive, but by the 1790s Lancaster's involvement in it was much diminished. From 1799 the smaller ports were barred by law from slaving and all Lancaster slave ships had to clear from Liverpool, London or Bristol. Official figures indicate that from 1785 to 1807 (when the slave trade was finally abolished) there was one ship yearly taking part in the African trade – presumably latterly via Liverpool.

The West Indies and Africa were not of course the only destinations of the Lancaster ships. They also went to the Baltic for timber, hemp and flax (for sail making), to North America for timber and to Portugal for wine. In addition there was an extremely extensive coastal trade, ranging from Glasgow, southern Scotland, Whitehaven and Liverpool in particular, to Bristol, London and Ireland. This usually involved over two hundred ships yearly.

At the end of the eighteenth century the larger ships, including most of the West Indian ones, docked at Glasson, whereupon their cargoes, mainly rum,

Details of some of the cargo on board the *Queen Charlotte* (John Thompson, Master) belonging to A. & J. Rawlinson of Lancaster and bound for Demerara in June 1798. It includes candles, 'sope', cheese and other foodstuffs. Hats were another major export from Lancaster, as were furniture and finished cloth.

WITH KIND PERMISSION OF LANCASHIRE LIBRARIES

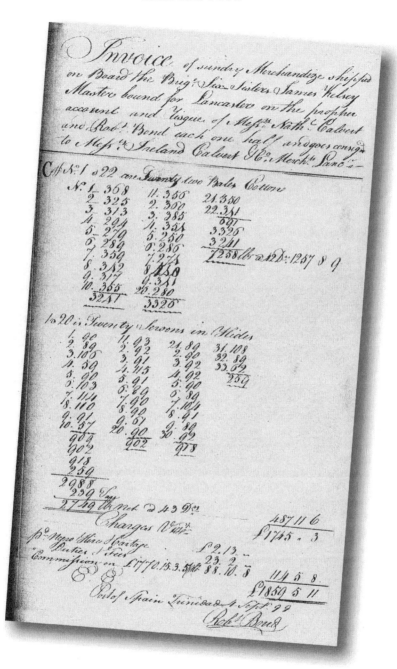

Details of some of the imports (mainly raw cotton) on board the *Six Sisters* from
Port of Spain, Trinidad to Lancaster for Ireland Calvert & Co. in September 1799.
Nathaniel Calvert subsequently went bankrupt. Rum, sugar, coffee and mahogany were
also major imports.

The last slave ship built in Lancaster identified by Andrew White as the *Trafalgar* of 1806. Built by Brockbanks, it belonged to William and Samuel Hinde. The former lived at Ellel Hall, Galgate and the latter at Dolphinholme although their business activities were by then mainly based in Liverpool. Both appear to have been buried in Lancaster Priory churchyard.

© LANCASTER CITY MUSEUM PART OF LANCASHIRE MUSEUMS

timber, sugar, cotton and coffee, then being taken upstream to St George's Quay by lighter or by road. Small ships, not exceeding two hundred tons, were often able to sail up the Lune to Lancaster itself, where they would presumably rest on the bed of the river at low tide.

Apart from the natural hazards of wind and weather during the war period an ever-present danger were the activities of French and later American privateers. Although the main fleets of France were defeated in a number of well-known set-piece engagements or kept bottled up in port by the Royal Navy blockade, the most terrible losses, involving many thousands of ships, were inflicted on the merchant vessels of this country. One calculation quoted by Schofield is that the French captured twelve times more merchant ships from the British than the other way round.[2] It has been possible to identify over thirty ships from Lancaster which were taken by the French (and occasionally by the Spanish) during the whole period of hostilities and after 1812 a further three or four captured by the Americans during the three-year war with that country. Details are set out in Appendix B.

The ships sailing to the West Indies were clearly most at risk. Those West Indies islands owned by the French and their enforced allies, the Dutch and Spanish, were a hot bed of privateers – ships licensed by their government to attack the commerce of the enemy. They were seldom a match for naval men-of-war, although they could often sail faster. They were, however, more

The Old Bridge at Lancaster still complete prior to the arch on the extreme left being demolished in 1802. Artist unknown but probably late eighteenth century.

© LANCASTER MARITIME MUSEUM PART OF LANCASHIRE MUSEUMS

heavily armed with a very much bigger crew and speedier than the average merchant ship which could usually do little against them, though, as we shall see, there were a number of successful defences. The 1790s was the worst period for the Lancaster ships, when the West Indies trade was at its heaviest, and the French still held on to their bases in Guadalupe and neighbouring islands. The convoy system was not yet properly operational and as a consequence merchant ships had to depend on their own efforts to fight off attacks. As a result the privateers reaped a golden harvest. Apart from the ships' captains, whom we will be looking at later, not much is known of the seamen who manned these ships. Not all can have come from Lancaster but clearly many did and, as already mentioned, Clark writing in 1807 estimates that there were approaching a thousand seamen from the town at the beginning of that century and the *Lancaster Gazette* quoted an actual figure of 1,605. Occasional

West Indian imports were sold regularly by auction throughout the period.

WITH KIND PERMISSION OF
LANCASHIRE LIBRARIES

glimpses do appear, such as James Ray, who was born in 1783. In 1830 he commenced legal proceedings relating to an application for poor law relief. He stated:

> When I was about eighteen years old [i.e., about 1801] I was bound apprentice to Mss Suarts, merchants in Lancaster, for four years to the sea service ...
> I served my first voyage to Dominica in the *Penelope*, Captain Parker from Glasson Dock ... I returned to Liverpool, where we discharged a cargo and then brought the vessel round to Glasson Dock. She remained at the dock there three months or thereabouts, during which time I slept sometimes at the dock, sometimes at Skerton [his home]. I sailed in the same vessel for four successive voyages and on my last voyage I was sent from Dominica to St Lucia in the ship *Thomas*, Captain Winder, with other apprentices. I left the *Thomas* at St Lucia before my time was out and I remained on shore longer than I ought to have done, afraid to return.'[3]

He appears to have returned to Liverpool at some stage and worked as a seaman before marrying, raising a family, being widowed and then finally returning to Lancaster.

One of the first Lancaster ships captured was the *Apollo*, taken in August 1794. Built in Lancaster in 1787, she was owned jointly by Edward Suart of Lancaster, George Suart of Dominica and Thomas Thompson and Richard Rowlandson of Barbados. The following months saw the capture of the *William*, belonging jointly to members of the related Worswick and Gillow families of Lancaster and Thomas Allman of St Kitts. The *William* was also a local vessel, having been built in 1785.

Some of the ships, such as the *Union*, had had a chequered history: originally a French ship, she was captured by a British privateer in July 1799 and taken into Martinique, then in British occupation, condemned as a prize and sent to Liverpool, where she was purchased by Thomas Walling Salisbury and William Sanderson, both merchants of Lancaster. Commanded by Captain Thomas, the *Union* was intercepted by the *La Mouche*, a French privateer from Bordeaux, and taken after a severe action of 3½ hours.

Obviously the taking of shipping could not avoid the loss of life. Another vessel also called the *Williams*, built at Glasgow in 1796, was registered at Lancaster in the April of the same year. She belonged to William Sanderson and Thomas Walling Salisbury, both merchants of Lancaster mentioned above. She sailed to the West Indies and was almost immediately taken by the French and carried into Guadalupe. Her captain, Thomas Strickland, was killed. The West Indies were clearly dangerous waters for merchant ships.

The *Alexander* was built in Lancaster in 1794; she was another vessel belonging to the Worswicks, who were both bankers and leading merchants of Lancaster; the Gillows also had a share in her, as did Thomas Allman of St Kitts. On route to the West Indies she was damaged in a gale before being intercepted by a French privateer of eighteen guns. In the bloody action which followed two crewmen and a passenger, Thomas Harrison, were killed and seven others wounded. As a consequence the *Alexander* was taken and carried into Guadalupe.[4]

Before 1801, when the first Lancaster newspaper began to be published, shipping information has to be obtained from other sources – mainly newspapers published in Liverpool or in Whitehaven. These give details of a number of successful defences mounted by Lancaster vessels. In March 1796, for example the *Atlantic*, commanded by Captain Nunns (a slave captain), encountered a French privateer brig carrying twelve or fourteen guns. The privateer had sought to disguise her identity by displaying British colours before hoisting 'the republican flag'. A violent action then followed 'on both sides with great guns when [they] came nearly alongside with a heavy fire of musketry, which continued without the least intermission for about an hour, when it thought proper to sheer off'. Both ships were badly damaged, particularly their sails, masts and rigging, and the *Atlantic* had two seamen badly wounded. The following year the *Atlantic*, this time commanded by Captain Thompson, was in action again. While in the Bay of Biscay on 30 May she was intercepted by a French privateer carrying eighteen to twenty guns.

> At four in the afternoon she got almost in our wake ... and came up with us very fast ... we bore up and run down towards her, hauled our wind again, she then fired a gun, hoisted French colours and gave us a broadside which we immediately returned and kept up a smart fire for about an hour. She then sheered off, apparently much in confusion, and men over the side.

The crew of the *Atlantic* escaped injury, but the ship itself was damaged both in the rigging and by a shot below the waterline, which caused serious flooding until it was stopped the following morning. Captain Thompson added: 'Our men behaved with great courage and steadiness, more so than could be expected as many had never been on board an armed ship before.'

In December 1798 the *Lancaster* was commanded by Captain Thomas Wilson, who was a part owner of the ship with a Joseph Sharpe, an anchor smith from Lancaster. On the 8th of that month Captain Wilson wrote to his co-owner describing how two days previously:

No. 174—Vol. IV.]

NOTICE IS HEREBY GIVEN,

To the OFFICERS and COMPANY of the SHIP
PARAGON,

WILLIAM HART, late Master,

Who were actually on board at
the CAPTURE of the SHIP
L'HARMONIE, and her CARGO,
the 26th day of July, 1803, bound
from New Orleans to Marseilles,
that they will be paid their respective, PROPOR-
TIONS of the PROCEEDS thereof, at the count-
ing-house of Messrs. RIDLEY and DODSON, in
Lancaster, on THURSDAY the 18th day of October
instant; and the shares not then demanded will be
ready, at the same place, every day afterwards (except Sundays) from ten till two o'clock.

LANCASTER, OCT. 8, 1804.

FOR DEMERARA.

THE SHIP
PARAGON,

PAUL REDMAYNE, Master;
Burthen 295 tons, mounts 20 guns;
now lying at Liverpool, and intended to join first
convoy from Cork. For freight or passage apply to
Messrs. RAWLINSON and BAGOTT, Liverpool; or
here, to

RIDLEY and DODSON.

LANCASTER, OCT. 4, 1804.

FOR BERBICE.

To sail with the FIRST CONVOY from CORK.

THE SHIP
L'HARMONIE,

WM. FRYER, Master.
Burthen 211 tons, mounts 10 guns,
is copper sheathed, and sails remarkably fast.
¶ For freight or passage apply to the said
Master; or

RIDLEY and DODSON.

LANCASTER, SEPT. 7, 1804.

TO BE SOLD BY AUCTION,

At SANDERSON, SALISBURY, and Co.'s office, in
Lancaster, on THURSDAY the 10th November
next, at twelve o'clock;

The beautiful, fast-sailing copper-
bottomed

S H I P
L'HARMONIE,

(Now lying in Glasson Dock)

Taken by the ship PARAGON, letter of marque,
WILLIAM HART, Master.

DIMENSIONS.

Length on Deck, 79 feet.
Breadth, 26 feet 1 inch.
Height between Decks, 5 feet.
Depth in the Hold, 2 feet 10½ inches.
Admeasures, 211 42-94th tons.
Has a Figure Head, and appears calculated for a
merchant ship, or a private ship of war.

After which will be SOLD,
PART of said VESSEL'S CARGO, in good condition, consisting of

109 Square Bales of New Orleans Cotton.

ABOUT

30 Tons fine Campeachy Logwood.
3 Hhds of French Claret.
24 Gallons of Rum.
1 Racoon Skins.
9 Deer Skins
Heavy Buffalo Hides.
Black Bear Skins.
Sheep Skin.
Hhds fine Biscuit Bread.
Barrels of Pork.
Elastic Steel Bandages.

B. The remainder of the Cargo, viz. 172 Bales
Orleans Cotton, and 34 Bales Deer Skins, may
ly be put up to public sale at same time.

For inventories, catalogues, and other par-
apply to
SANDERSON, SALISBURY, and CO.
Brokers.
LANCASTER, OCT. 28, 1803.

Sale details of the French prize *L'Harmonie* then safely at Glasson Dock.

From the *Lancaster Gazette* 13 October 1804, indicating the share out of the prize
money following the capture of *L'Harmonie* by the *Paragon* the previous year. Both
ships continued in the West India Trade.

We discovered a ship ahead, standing to the southward. At eight o'clock she tacked towards us and although she had English colours on I made her plainly an enemy mounting twenty guns, many full of men. Our guns were well loaded with round [shot] and grape [shot] and the men at their quarters when she came alongside hauled the English colours down and hoisted French ... After engaging us two hours he had enough of it and hauled his colours down but our vessel being in a shattered position without a brace or any rope to get the yards round, he took advantage of it and made off ... We had one man killed and four wounded and the sails awry, much torn and cut.

The ship survived the first part of the wars and was wrecked off Jamaica in 1802. Captain Wilson will be met with again.

By 1801 something of a stalemate had been reached in the conduct of the war. Notwithstanding a series of military coalitions put together by the British prime minister, William Pitt, French armies (despite some defeats) had triumphed over the Austrian and Russian empires and were now the supreme military power on the continent. British military intervention had not been successful, despite the seizure of some of the colonial possessions belonging to the French and their allies. Twice British armies had been driven out of the Low Countries and only in Egypt had there been any major success. At sea, of course, it was another matter, with the Royal Navy remaining virtually unchallenged against the combined efforts of France, Spain, Holland and Denmark. Peace in 1801 suited everybody, and most but not all of what had been gained by British conquest was handed back to the original owners. The preliminaries of peace were signed in October 1801 and news of this caused general rejoicings in Lancaster. Of course, it was many months before the news spread to other parts of the globe, and consequently the convoy system remained in force and local shipping remained at risk. During this time two Lancaster ships, the *Venerable*, under Captain Croft, and the *Richard*, under Captain Thompson, were attacked and taken by Spanish privateers. The latter sustained five killed, including the first and second mates, and the same number of wounded. The ship was taken into the Spanish colonial port of Cartagena and the surviving members of the crew were not sent to Jamaica until January 1802.

The 1801 cessation of hostilities – the Peace of Amiens – turned out to be only a breathing space in the seemingly endless war between Britain and France. As far as Lancaster was concerned, it did coincide with a marked slackening in overseas trade, particularly with the West Indies. In 1799 fifty-seven ships arrived from that part of the world, falling to twenty in 1801, and to just eight the following year – the lowest figure for decades. There was a modest improvement to twelve ships in 1803, and thereafter the figure remained fairly consistently in the teens, with a high of twenty in 1809. As soon as the war was over in 1815 the trade collapsed, for reasons we shall explore later.[5] The coasting trade, by contrast, remained fairly constant – usually involving over 200 ships yearly – indicative of its vital importance, particularly in the carriage of heavy and bulky items.

The Peace of Amiens did not endure, ended by a mixture of French bad faith and British stubbornness. In retrospect it can be seen that a renewal of hostilities was inevitable. A formal declaration of war from Britain followed on 15 May 1803, although this had been anticipated by the calling out of the militia in March and the remobilisation of the Navy.

One suspects that the mood in Lancaster was one of anger and resignation and the feeling that once again local seamen were to bear the brunt of the war. In this second phase of hostilities this turned out not to be the case, although some of the best-known events occurred during this period. The *Lancaster Gazette* of 11 June reported the sailing of 'the *Eliza* letter of marque of 18 guns Captain Moon for Dominica' and some four weeks later, 'on Wednesday last the *Mars*, letter of marque Wilson, carrying 20 guns, 24 and 12-pounders, sailed in company with the *Paragon* letter of marque Hart, carrying 20 guns, 24 and 9 pounders, for Barbados.' Not long after leaving the Lune the *Paragon* was responsible for one of the best-known incidents of Lancaster maritime history. On 25 July she captured the French ship *La Harmonie*, with a cargo of cotton, timber and buffalo hides. She was brought into Glasson Dock by William Fryer, the mate of the *Paragon*, and there sold. The French ship, which had not heard of the war, was carrying seven passengers, four of whom arrived in her. As far as is known, no further French prizes were actually brought into Lancaster during the war, although the twenty-gun *Thomas* letter of marque, Captain Richard Winder, was having a successful run. On 13 August the *Gazette* reported that: 'A vessel from the Havannah, detained by the ship *Thomas*, Captain Winder, has arrived at Beerhaven [Ireland]', and again at the end of October 1803, 'The *St Augusteen* ... captured by the *Thomas* of this port, laden with hides and ostrich feathers, arrived at Liverpool on Sunday.' Finally, on 31 December 1803, the *Gazette* recorded: 'The *Thomas*, Winder of this port at Barbados and Berbice. About eighty leagues to windward of Barbados she was attacked by three schooner privateers whom she beat off after a smart action, carrying away the topmast of one of them.'

Despite these various encounters, it is clear that the tempo post-1803 had declined, that the disasters of the 1790s were not being repeated, and that

> **WANTS A PLACE,**
> *IN A GENTLEMAN'S FAMILY,*
>
> A YOUNG MAN of COLOUR, lately from the West Indies; he has been accustomed to wait at table, and is willing to make himself useful to his employer. He speaks good English.
> *§* An excellent character will be given by inquiring at STEEL, JOHNSTONE, and Co.'s, Penny-street, Lancaster.
> JULY 17, 1807.

The West Indies connection brought strangers into Lancaster. This man was not a slave, and at the very least would receive a small wage and probably accommodation.

WITH KIND PERMISSION OF LANCASHIRE LIBRARIES

far fewer ships were being captured. One can only guess at the reasons but perhaps the fact that there were many fewer Lancaster ships sailing, perhaps a more sophisticated convoy system and the gradual elimination of the French privateering bases in the West Indies – their last West Indian strongholds Martinique and Guadalupe fell in 1809 and 1810, respectively. Perhaps also the privateers were concentrating on the Channel and North Sea traffic and this to some extent spared the shipping crossing the Atlantic. A number of ships captured by the enemy were so fortunate as to be recaptured – such as the *Fortitude* in the summer of 1807, with four killed and eight wounded. The *Valentine* was taken on its way home from Jamaica in the same year and the *Eliza* likewise in 1812, having survived a brush with the enemy off Ireland the previous year. Towards the end of 1813 the *John of Gaunt*, Captain Peter Inglis, had the misfortune to be taken by the French forty-gun frigate *Clorinde*, which had avoided the British blockade and had gone on a commerce raiding cruise. The crew were not detained, but the *John of Gaunt* was set on fire and sunk.[6] Between 1812 and 1814 three further Lancaster ships were captured by the Americans. The war with France ended in April 1814 with the capture of Paris by the allies and the abdication of Bonaparte. The thousands of prisoners in French hands – mainly seamen – could now be returned, including those from Lancaster. The war with America still continued until the beginning of 1815 and as news of both events took a long time to travel vigilance had to be maintained and the convoy system continued. Clashes with American privateers continued throughout the spring of that year and were duly reported in the *Lancaster Gazette*. The last such incident appears to have taken place on 3 April 1815, when, 'the *James* Simpson of this port from St Thomas and San Domingo at Liverpool after being plundered ... on her passage between the two former places by the American privateer *Hollins*.'

The dramatic events of the Hundred Days with Napoleon back on the throne of France, the Battle of Waterloo and the second occupation of Paris do not seem to have given rise to fresh privateering. Both Guadalupe and Martinique had been returned to France in 1814 and the former had to be recaptured all over again. It was then re-returned to France. The long struggle at sea was finally over and the Lancaster ships could sail peacefully wherever they chose. However, the glory days of the exotic trade with the West Indies were now also virtually over, never to be revived.

It is obvious that the shipping trade from Lancaster involved many people although how many is not entirely clear. As already mentioned, Clark writing in 1807 calculated that in 1801 there were probably just under 1,000 seamen so employed. The census of 1811 mentions families employed in the army, navy and merchants' vessels as only sixty-nine. This relates to families and not individuals and is surely something of a substantial under-estimate, this belief being tentatively supported by the preponderance of female residents revealed in both sets of census figures. Be that as it may, the identities of the seamen of Lancaster are, largely speaking, unknown but in respect of some of the ships' captains it has been possible to map out some part of their careers, which were often dangerous, always demanding, and which required a high degree of seamanship. Some of the more prominent ships' captains of Lancaster are worthy of a more detailed study.

The Old Town Hall in Market Square, Lancaster.
Used as such from 1783 until 1909.

· CHAPTER FIVE ·

The sea captains

William Hart

One of the best known of Lancaster sailors was William Hart. He was born in 1763 and he is believed to have originated from the Furness area of Lancashire, where the surname is still common. Details of his early life are unknown, but his first command was the *Rawlinson*, which belonged to the brothers Abram and John Rawlinson, leading West Indian merchants of Lancaster. For five years from 1788 he sailed regularly to and from Granada. Then in 1793 he took over the *Liberty*, until she was captured the following year. The circumstances of this capture are somewhat bizarre. Apparently the *Liberty* had been intercepted by a French privateer of fourteen guns and 'full of men'. After an engagement lasting some time the Frenchman was beaten off. At about eleven o'clock at night the ship's gunner and another man went down into the powder room, which 'unfortunately caught fire and the after part of the ship immediately blew up. The remaining part of the ship was soon in a blaze which continued burning till nearly eleven o'clock the following morning.' Captain Hart and two of his crew ('much scorched') were picked up by the privateer and put on board a ship bound for Liverpool, where one of them died. While recovering from his injuries Captain Hart would then no doubt have time to reflect upon the fate of his late ship and also on the possibly negligent conduct of the gunner or his assistant, who were also blown overboard by the original explosion and lost, as were two other members of the crew. By November 1796 Hart had recovered and was now captain of the *Hector* sailing to Martinique before transferring to the *Fortitude* in 1800. His next few voyages were to either Demerara or Granada. He took over command of the newly built *Paragon* in 1802. She was built by Brockbanks of Lancaster, was three-masted and displaced 295 tons. She received a substantial armament of twenty guns. Her owners Ridley and Dodson of Lancaster applied for and obtained letters of marque, which entitled the ship to seek out and capture enemy merchant ships. As we have already seen, she captured the French ship *La Harmonie* soon after war broke out again in 1803. Later the same year the *Paragon* was in action again, with Captain Hart writing to his owners in Lancaster from Barbados on 16 August:

> Yesterday morning eighteen leagues to the windward of this island I fell in with a French schooner privateer of twelve guns and about a hundred men, who lay the *Paragon* on board on the starboard quarter and after a desperate action of nearly an hour he got disentangled and made off quite a wreck. During the engagement he made several attempts to throw his men on board the *Paragon* but was resolutely repulsed by our small crew. Our heavy guns on the quarterdeck with grape shot made dreadful carnage amongst the crew of the privateer, her decks were all covered with dead bodies before she got from alongside and her scubbards ran with blood. I am sorry to add that of our small brave crew two were killed and seven wounded.

The battered *Paragon* arrived safely back in the Lune on 28 May 1804.

William Hart took her to Demerara again twice before handing over to Paul Redmayne in 1805. Captain Hart had her back for a voyage in 1806 to Berbice but in 1808 he transferred to the fourteen-gun *Jane*, again going to Berbice, the *Paragon* being sold to Liverpool owners. Captain Hart's last ship appears to have been the *Neptune* (formerly the *Neptuno*), a Prussian ship taken over by the British authorities during the brief period of hostilities with Prussia. She initially sailed from Liverpool, was armed with sixteen guns and carried letters of marque and traded with either Berbice or Surinam, a recently captured Dutch colony. The *Neptune's* return from the latter place to Lancaster in 1811 seems to mark the end of William Hart's seagoing career, with the *Neptune* being offered for sale. He died aged sixty-four in November 1827, and was survived by a wife, two sons and three daughters. By his will, which he had made in 1810, he left his whole estate to his wife for life and 'chaste widowhood' and thereafter to his two sons, Thomas and William, in succession and then to his other children.[1]

As far as the famous *Paragon* is concerned, she was subsequently re-registered with Liverpool owners, the captain being a Thomas Clint. Both *Paragon* and her companion vessel, the *William*, were captured by the American privateer *Grand Turk* of sixteen guns and 130 men in April 1813 while on a voyage to Buenos Aires. However, she seems to have been recaptured because she was in Halifax, Nova Scotia, in November of that year.[2]

Thomas Wilson

Thomas Wilson was born in 1769 and subsequently lived in Chapel Street, Lancaster, with his wife, Alice. Nothing is known of his early life. His first command appears to have been the ship *Lancaster*, and he sailed her regularly to the West Indies between 1797 and 1801. Wilson's voyages usually were to Jamaica, although there was one trip to Martinique in 1798. As we have already seen, he fought off a French privateer in the Irish Sea in the summer of that year. After the wrecking of the *Lancaster* off Jamaica in 1802, he took over the twenty-gun *Mars* in 1803 and sailed her twice to the Danish West Indian island of St Thomas. In 1805 he got a new ship, the *Neptune*, owned by Thomas Burrow and Thomas Mason of Lancaster. The *Neptune* (not to be confused with the ex-Prussian *Neptuno* mentioned previously) had been built by Brockbanks at their Lancaster yard in the same year and she was intended for the West India trade. She sailed regularly either to Tortola or St Thomas, sometimes making two voyages per year, with a crew varying between nineteen and twenty-seven men.

On his first voyage, in the company of two ships from Liverpool, they fell in with the American ship *Huntress*, a prize to the Spanish privateer, *Maria*, from Puerto Rico. The *Huntress* was retaken, apparently without difficulty, and brought into Lancaster. Captain Wilson's last voyage with the *Neptune* began on 15 April 1809, when he left the Lune bound for St Thomas. On the 22nd of that month he fell in with a French navy corvette, mounting sixteen guns and with a crew of 145 men. After an engagement of half an hour the *Neptune* was compelled to surrender. Captain Wilson and most of his crew were taken on board the French ship, leaving behind the four passengers, a Mr Burrow, a Mr Hewitson, a Captain Waller and a Captain Woodhouse, plus two ship's boys together with a French prize master and a prize crew of sixteen Spaniards. The *Neptune* was thoroughly plundered, even down to the passengers' watches and their clothing. The two ships then set course for Corunna in the north of Spain, then in the occupation of the French army, but became separated in a gale. The account in the *Lancaster Gazette* tells the rest of the story:

> From the knowledge Mr Burrow had of the French and Spanish language it was soon discovered that several of the Spaniards were dissatisfied with the French prize master, which circumstances induced the passengers to attempt the recovery of the ship, in which they were fortunately successful ... Captain Waller took command and they arrived safe at Madeira on the 5th of May, where they received assistance from Captain Sagar of His Majesty's ship *Raleigh*.

The *Neptune* later returned to Lancaster and resumed West Indian voyages under a Captain Johnson but a very different fate was reserved for the crew of the *Neptune*. Apart from Captain Wilson himself they were sent to the French fortress at Briancon, where they remained as prisoners of war until December the following year. Seven of them finally ended up at the prison camp at Arras, where presumably they remained until released on the general peace in April, 1814.[3]

As for Thomas Wilson, he found himself confined in the fortress of Verdun. This prison was reserved for naval and military officers, merchant navy skippers and also for the civilian detainees who had been kept in France after the breakdown of the Peace of Amiens in 1803. However, this obviously tough and resourceful seaman had other ideas and on 15 January 1814, the *Lancaster Gazette* was able (with tantalisingly few details) to report:

> On Wednesday morning Captain Thomas Wilson who was captured on the ship *Neptune* of this port ... arrived in this town on making escape from bondage ... with five others ... He suffered many privations after leaving Verdun, having been several weeks from that place before they got on board a King's ship, and had many remarkable and hair-raising escapes.

Captain Wilson subsequently returned to the sea, commanding the ship *Thomas* for the next three years, taking her to St Croix, Philadelphia and Antigua. He died at Lancaster in August 1819, aged sixty years. He left all of his estate to his 'dear wife', who survived until 1845. He was not a rich man, his total possessions not exceeding eight hundred pounds.[4] Like Captain Hart, he is buried in the Lancaster Priory churchyard.[5]

Henry Coupland

Captain Henry Coupland was born in 1768. He probably came from a Lancaster family and was admitted a freeman of the town at the early age of sixteen. Nothing is known of his seafaring career until 1797, when he was appointed captain of the *Clio*. This was a three-masted ship of 266 tons, built in Lancaster and owned by Edward and Nicholas Salisbury and Josiah Baxendale, all of Lancaster, together with another owner from Martinique.

Captain Coupland sailed the *Clio* regularly until 1802, invariably to Martinique, sometimes making two trips in a year. Between 1802 and 1807 there is a gap in the records at Lancaster, and it seems possible that during this period he sailed from Liverpool; certainly the *Clio's* registration was transferred to Liverpool in 1805. By 1807 or about then he was in command of the ten-gun *Richard* sailing from Lancaster to Jamaica, followed by three voyages in the three-masted *Thomas* to Dominica. Captain Coupland's last ship appears to have been the 370-ton *Lune*, launched in February 1810. She was owned jointly by owners in Liverpool and Lancaster and was built by Caleb, Smith & Co. at their yard in Skerton. Captain Coupland sailed regularly to the West Indies with her, destinations being either Granada or Demerara. His last voyage was in 1814, after which Captain James Bloor took over the ship. This leaving of the sea seems to coincide more or less with his marriage (probably a second one), followed by the birth of his children. He presumably decided that his new responsibilities took precedence over his shipping career.

Not dying until 1858, when he was then ninety years of age, Henry Coupland had the benefit of an obituary in the local paper. The *Lancaster Guardian* wrote:

> During the palmiest days of Lancaster he was engaged in the West
> India trade and was known as a successful, prudent and much esteemed
> commander. During the war with France ... on one occasion he was captured
> by the enemy. To add to mortification of this event, some special meal which
> he had been preparing for the Christmas celebration was also seized by the
> Frenchmen and added to their own table ... however, an English frigate hove
> in sight and succeeded in restoring Captain Coupland and his crew to liberty.

After retiring from the sea Captain Coupland became quite prominent in Lancaster. He was appointed a member of the Board of Guardians which administered the poor law, as well as serving on the Corporation and the Port Commission, where his knowledge of nautical matters was of great use. Socially, he was a member of the Philippi Society, a group of leading citizens of the time which met informally at the Black Horse Hotel in Common Garden Street. He lived at 22 Cable Street.

Henry Coupland married Emma Johnson in 1812 and their son Richard Coupland was born two years later. The latter was subsequently apprenticed to the firm of Gillows and later he was one of the principals of Bell and Coupland, furniture makers of Lancaster. Captain Coupland's great-grandson, also called Henry Coupland, was killed at Ypres on the 24 April 1915, at the age of twenty years, while serving in the King's Own. He was the last of the male line.

John Charnley

Of all the Lancaster sea captains John Charnley has become the best known. He was almost a legend in his own lifetime and the boys of Lancaster Grammar School used to sing a song about his exploits. The reason for Captain Charnley's fame is the action which took place between his ship, *Thetis*, and the French privateer *Bonaparte* in 1804 in the West Indies. In 1869 a series of extracts were printed, which were taken from the pages of the *Lancaster Gazette*, which, as we know, started in 1801. These extracts were titled 'Leaves from Local History'. This has proved a great boon to local historians but a comparison with the original *Lancaster Gazette* indicates that the 1869 publication is at its best very incomplete and much of interest and value still remains to be discovered and transcribed.

One thing, however, which did appear in Leaves from Local History was an account by Captain Charnley of the events of 8 November 1804, when off Barbados in the company of two other ships, the *Ceres* and the *Penelope*, he fell in with the French privateer *Bonaparte*. A bloody contest then followed, with the *Bonaparte* making four attempts to board *Thetis*, each one being repulsed. The vessels then parted company, exchanged broadsides, with the privateer sailing off with a favourable wind. On board the *Thetis* two of the crew were killed and five severely wounded. As far as the *Bonaparte* was concerned, three days later she was taken by the *Cyane* sloop of war and carried into Antigua. Her captain reported: 'We found the *Bonaparte* in a very shattered condition, she had lost her foremast, and bowsprit in action with three English letters of marque three days prior to her capture.'

Captain Charnley was very rightly rewarded for his successful defence and he was presented with a piece of plate, valued £60, suitably inscribed by the inhabitants of Dominica. His crew were given sums of money – graded according to rank – from £12 for Mr Freres, chief mate, a similar sum for the families of two men killed, £8 for the second mate and each of the eight wounded and to the thirty-one unwounded survivors £4 each. On his return to Lancaster Captain Charnley was made an honorary freeman of the town. Captain Charnley is unusual, in as much as he appears to have only captained the *Thetis* and sailed her then continuously from 1796 to 1805, when he apparently retired from the sea at the early age of thirty-five. He married shortly afterwards. He later lived at 2 Castle Park, and also owned what is now the Giant Axe field. Captain Charnley died in 1834, aged sixty-four, and is buried at Mytton in Yorkshire. His tombstone is still just decipherable. He was succeeded by an only son, who died intestate and who had built Thetis

House, which still stands adjacent to the Giant Axe field in West Road, Lancaster. Charnley Street is nearby. There were no direct descendants. Incidentally, his former chief mate, Robert Frears (or Freres), died of severe wounds received during his unsuccessful defence of the *Fortitude* (of which he was captain) some three years later when attacked by two French privateers off St Domingo.

A brief account of the life of John Charnley was written in 1916 by T. Cann Hughes, a local historian and sometime town clerk of Lancaster.[6] Apparently he had made every effort to trace the piece of silver from the inhabitants of Dominica but without success. No doubt it still exists and it would be nice if its whereabouts could be discovered. As for the *Thetis* herself, she was sold in 1806 to Samuel Hinde of Liverpool and William Hinde of Ellel Hall at Galgate and sailed from Liverpool thereafter. She was finally sold to London owners in 1810. [7]

Davis Thompson

Nothing is known of Davis Thompson until he became captain of the 260-ton *Harriet* in 1806. She was another of Brockbanks' ships and had been launched three years previously. In December 1806 he was attacked in the West Indies by a French privateer of ten guns, which he beat off 'after an engagement of two and a half hours'. On the way back to Lancaster from Berbice in the company of the *Alexander* of Liverpool they had the misfortune to fall in with the French privateer *L'Alert* of 20 guns and 200 men. A severe engagement lasting an hour followed in which the *Alexander* suffered four men killed and five, including her captain, wounded. *L'Alert* then turned her attention on the *Harriet* and a further conflict of forty minutes followed in which the French ship was now assisted by the captured *Alexander*. The *Lancaster Gazette* reported:

> The *Harriet* continued to engage both ships until her sails and rigging were much cut, Captain Thompson shot through the thigh with a musket ball and several of his crew wounded he struck his colours.

The mate of the *Harriet* and some of the crew were put by the privateer on board an American ship bound for Philadelphia, but the remainder were rescued some ten days later when the *Harriet* and the privateer were taken by a Royal Navy ship and carried into Grenada. On 13 June 1807 the *Harriet* arrived safely at Glasson with its cargo still intact.

HOMEWARD BOUND,

Or, Huzza for Glasson:

A SONG,

(Written by a Sailor belonging to the Port of Lancaster.)

OH what pleasure we have, with what joy cry amain,
When in sight of old Ireland we arrive once again,
When from the West Indies the whole fleet are bound,
And heaving our lead, we first strike Irish Ground.

CHORUS.

Bound for Glasson, huzza for Glasson!
Let us all sing in praise of JOHN LAMB's parlour door!

Now there's some bound to London and some bound to the
Clyde,
There's some bound to Dublin and Bristol beside,
There's some bound to Liverpool, round the Black Rock,
But we're bound to that beautiful place Glasson Dock.
And it's oh for Glasson! &c.

Now the wind's from the westward, it blows a fresh gale,
By this we are nearly abreast of Kinsale ;
And for to bend Cables all hands are at work,
Till we get clear of danger—we call that past Cork.
And it's oh for Glasson ! &c.

Then you'll see brother Pat alongside he will come,
To exchange his potatoes for a bottle of rum;
And kindly entreats us then for to heave to,
But no, no, Mr. Paddy that never will do,
For we are bound to Glasson, &c

Then the night coming on E. S. E. then we steer,
And carry all sail the old STERLING will bear :
About 12 at night there's the Hook light we see,
And long before daylight we round the Saltee.
And it's oh for Glasson ! &c

Then its sixty good miles we have run thro' the night,
And early next morning there's Tusker in sight ;
When the water's as smooth and as red as a bead,
Then we steer our course straight till we see Holy Head.
And it's oh for Glasson ! &c.

When to the Welch Coast we then do draw nigh,
Old Bardsey's the next land that we do espy ;
Then you'll see several Vessels there coming down
Saying "what pleasure you boys have, who are homeward boun
" Perhaps to Glasson," &c

Now the most is to get a good sight of the Stack,
With Royals and Stay-sails and all we can pack ;
Look out well a-head, there, and on the lee bow,
For I think it's near time, boys, we should see it now.
Huzza for Glasson ! &c

And this is accomplished about eight at night,
When a Sailor proclaims that he can see the light,
Crying " yonder it is, now, I see it quite plain,
" For it goes out a-while and it comes in again."
And its oh for Glasson ! &c

Oh how happy the Crew and each tar how much blest !
When we're off Holy Head and the wind is at West ;
It drives all our sorrows and dull cares away,
Expecting to see all our dear friends the next day.
All about Glasson, &c

Then we alter our course to East and by Nor,
And crack her away for the Lancashire Shore ;
But the night being long we must keep a look out,
That our Ship before day-light, may get too far a-head.
And it's oh for Glasson ! &c.

Then we heave our Ship to until break of day,
Till we think it's near time for to bear away,
Under easy Sail, till the morning is clear,
Then what a number of beautiful objects appear,
All about Glasson ! &c.

The first is Black Comb with his wintry cap on,
There's the Bluff-end of Highfield and th' Steeple in one,
There's Rostal Land-mark, on the star-board side ;
Tis low water now, with a twenty foot tide.
Then Huzza for Glasson ! &c.

Then the thund'ring reports of our guns they are heard,
All the way from the Land-mark unto the church-yard,
Where a number of people there standing you'll see,
Very busy consulting what Ship it will be,
That's coming to Glasson, &c.

Some say it's the Thomas as sure as you live,
For her high quarter deck I can clearly perceive ;
But it soon after appears that it's blue, white, and red.
And its oh for Glasson ! &c.

Then we run up a little way nearer the Buoy,
And fire eight Guns to wish them much joy ;
It's now two hours flood and the tide making fast,
Ah ! ah ! ROBERT COTTY, you're coming at last,
To take us to Glasson! &c.

Then to hear all the news due attention is paid,
And listening like pigs for to hear what is said ;
Says ROBERT, " I think there is little at all,
" But the folks are o' weel about th' Dock and Pier Hall,
" And all about Glasson," &c.

Then we pass the first Buoy, and soon all the rest,
Until that the perch we are nearly abreast ;
" Then stand by your braces," old ROBERT does say,
And up with your helm and keep her away ;
Right for Glasson ! &c.

What a number of people you'll see then flock down,
With horses and chaises, and gigs from the town ;
There's old JOHN LAMB syling with snuff box in hand,
Crying " come, come, every man now, and pull her to land :
" For to get her in Glasson," &c.

Now the Ship she's inside of JOHN LAMB's parlour door,
Then up to Pier Hall we must go to be sure :
When we find our dear girls come fast down in great stile,
And each graciously welcomes us home with a smile ;
" You'r welcome to Glasson," &c.

And now since the Ship is got safe into dock,
You'll see how the folks will on board of her flock,
Saying, " Sailors you're all now welcome safe home,
" We're come for to taste a lile sup of your rum."
" That you've brought to Glasson," &c.

(CLARK, Printer, Lancaster.)

The main interest in this song is the light that it throws on the approach of oceangoing ships to Glasson and the subsequent docking. Also of interest is the reaction of local inhabitants to the sound of the ships' guns which together with the ships' flags helped to identify the vessel in question. The song is not dated, but internal evidence suggests either 1813 or 1814.

Now, however, Davis Thompson's luck began to run out. Presumably having recovered from his wound, he left Liverpool on 14 February 1808 in the company of the *Thomas*, Captain Coupland (also of Lancaster) bound for the West Indies. Almost immediately they ran into a severe gale and the *Harriet* struck West Hoyle Bank. The masts were cut away and many of the ship's guns thrown overboard but to no avail and she sank off the Point of Ayre on the North Wales coast. The *Lancaster Gazette* continued:

> The second mate together with five of the crew and apprentices at the wish of the captain had previously left the ship in a small boat to get assistance from the land which they reached with difficulty. All the remainder of the ship's company, including Captain Thompson, the Chief Mate, twenty-two crew members and two passengers (one being a Mr Walmesley of Lancaster) were drowned.[8]

Other captains

Of course, there were in addition other ships' captains who sailed from Lancaster, and their names occur frequently in the columns of the *Lancaster Gazette* or other documents of the time. There was Captain William Tresure of Lancaster, who made many voyages to Martinique, Trinidad and Demerara in the *Edwards*, the *Adelphi* and the *Aid*. He died at sea on his way home from Tortola on board the *Abram* in 1807, aged sixty-four. According to the *Lancaster Gazette*, 'he had been many years in the employ of several merchants of this town whom he had served faithfully and had gained the esteem of all who knew him'. His daughter Bella married Leonard Redmayne of another Lancaster and Liverpool seafaring family. Redmayne had a very successful career in business, taking control of the Gillows furniture business when that family withdrew from active participation in the trade. He was the first chairman of the Lancaster Banking Company in 1826, and was also mayor of Lancaster. His grandson, a dragoon officer, was killed in the Indian Mutiny.[9] Leonard Redmayne had what were probably two cousins – Paul Redmayne and another Leonard Redmayne. Both captained ships sailing from Lancaster as well as Liverpool.

A very fortunate captain was James Moon, who was master of the *Alfred* of Lancaster. In 1801, in the company of two Liverpool ships, he intercepted and captured the *La Galga*, a Spanish ship, *en route* from the River Plate to Cadiz. *La Galga* was carrying a cargo of hides, cocoa, indigo and copper bars, rumoured to be worth some £50,000. For some reason the *Alfred*'s share of the cargo or its value was not distributed to her crew until early 1812. Captain Moon died at sea in the same year.

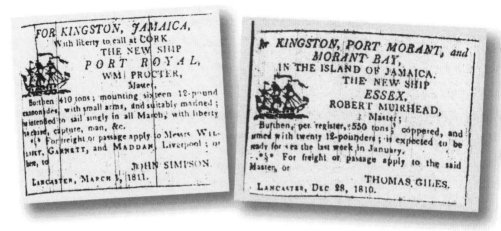

Two brand new Lancaster ships. *The Port Royal* built by Smiths at their yard in Skerton and, the *Essex* from Brockbank's yard Cable Street – both for the West India trade.

Other captains included William Procter of the sixteen-gun *Port Royal*, built by Smiths at Skerton, and James Bragg of the *Eliza*. In 1811 both had brushes with French privateers, in the Channel and off Ireland respectively. Nicholas Carter sailed the *Pusey Hall* for Moores of Lancaster, to and from Jamaica for several years up to and after the end of the war. Early in 1815 he was attacked in the West Indies by two American privateers, which after a two-hour engagement he managed to beat off. His owners, James Moore & Co. of Gage Street, Lancaster, must have been very pleased to receive a letter from Rear Admiral Durham anchored in Carlisle Bay, Barbadoes, the Naval Commander in the West Indies, as follows: 'Gentlemen, I congratulate you on having such a Captain and crew on board the ship *Pusey Hall*: she was attacked by two American privateers on Sunday the 26th inst. and succeeded in beating them off. She is now safe at anchor in this bay. I am, Gentlemen, Your obedient servant C. Durham.'[10]

One should not forget some other names, such as William Neale, in the *Vine*, whose regular run was to Oporto in the wine trade, and William Kellet, who sailed the *Langton* in the timber trade to Riga and Memel. Perhaps more forgettable was John Nunns, Lancaster's last slave captain, who died at sea and was buried in Trinidad in 1807, the year the British slave trade became unlawful, but whose memorial stone remains to this day in St John's churchyard, Lancaster. Obviously, he had no scruples in taking part in a trade which by the early nineteenth century had become abhorrent to a majority of people in the country. He was a tough, experienced seaman who was relied upon by his Lancaster backers to produce results both off the west coast of Africa as well as in the slave markets of the West Indies. Indeed, in July 1805 Captain Nunns was reported as at Surinam from Angola and 'selling there'.

His last ship was *The Johns* of eighteen guns, built by Brockbanks in 1800 and called after himself and his two Lancaster backers, John Lowther and John Cumpsty. After his death, the ship was sold to Liverpool owners and wrecked off the coast of Africa in December 1809 – possibly while involved in illegal slaving. Captain Nunns was quite well off at his death, owning house property both in Skerton (where he lived) and Storth, near Arnside. In addition he had personal property amounting to over £3,000. He was survived by his wife Sarah and children – one of whom married the daughter of Captain Nicholas Carter.[11]

Compulsory service in the Militia was not popular for many.

ABSCONDED,

From Yealand Redmayne, in the county of Lancaster, the latter end of January last;

WILLIAM RAWLINSON, ballotted into the MILITIA. The said William Rawlinson is about five feet nine inches high, light hair, and light complexion; about twenty-five years of age, and has of late followed the occupation of a labourer.

⁂ Whoever will apprehend him, will receive a REWARD of FORTY SHILLINGS, by giving notice thereof to JOHN HARRISON, constable for Yealand Redmayne.

YEALAND REDMAYNE, JUNE 25, 1803.

WHEREAS JOHN TAYLOR, of Freckleton, near Kirkham, Lancashire, weaver, ballotted to serve in the Supplementary Militia, has absented himself from duty:

This is to give Notice,

That whoever will apprehend and detain the said John Taylor, on or before the 15th of July, 1803, shall receive a reward of FIVE POUNDS, from the Overseer of Freckleton —He is about five feet five inches high; of a dark complexion; thirty-six years of age; has served in the Royal Lancashire Volunteers; and has a wife and one child.

In the very busy coastal trade was William Cleminson of Lancaster, firstly the master of the charmingly named *Tyger* and then the *Lark*, a Brockbank ship which he sailed between Lancaster and Liverpool on a very regular basis throughout the whole of the war period.

In addition to the Lancaster sea captains whose careers we have already examined, there is another – Thomas Greenwood – about whose life we know considerably more, and as a consequence he deserves a chapter to himself.

· CHAPTER SIX ·

The last voyage of
Captain Thomas Greenwood

Thomas Greenwood was born in 1758, the son of Robert and Anne Greenwood of Fox Tree, Kirkby Lonsdale. In later life he prepared a written account of 'the principal events in the life of Captain Thomas Greenwood'. We no longer know where this valuable manuscript is, but fortunately large parts were copied out in the late nineteenth century and published in the local newspaper, probably by Anthony Hewitson, a journalist with a great interest in local history.[1] Unfortunately, Hewitson, like his contemporary 'Cross Fleury' (Robert Rigbye), never gave references in his writings or provided proper details of his sources. However, there is no particular reason to doubt the accuracy of this particular account (notwithstanding editing and improving the spelling) and certain details can be substantiated from other records.

Thomas Greenwood was educated at Whittington school and later at a school in Kellet, where we are told he learned the elements of navigation. In 1772 at the age of fourteen he was bound apprentice to John Watson & Co., merchants of Lancaster, for a term of six years on board wages only. His first ship was the 150-ton *Watson*, Captain Haythornthwaite, and in her he sailed to St Kitts and Dominica in the West Indies. Further voyages followed and by 1778, then out of apprenticeship, he was appointed second mate and two years later first mate. In 1781 Thomas Greenwood had his first, albeit temporary, command – the fourteen-gun *Comet*. This ship was apparently registered in Lancaster but 'belonged' to Antigua. She sailed out of Liverpool, where she was fitted out as a letter of marque. He returned in her to Antigua, before going to the Danish island of St Thomas, where she was sold. He then shipped as a passenger to a neutral Danish ship to return to Antigua but unfortunately it was intercepted by the French fleet commanded by the Admiral Conte De Grasse, taken into the Dutch isle St Eustatia, where her cargo of timber was confiscated. According to Greenwood, he thereby lost 'Six hundred hard dollars and all his clothes'. After three weeks in captivity he was exchanged and returned to Antigua, before coming back to this country in the brig *Morson* as chief mate.

In October 1782 the *Morson* left Lancaster again *en route* for Tortola. She carried no guns and was consequently an easy victim for the American privateer *Rennette* of Philadelphia commanded by an ex-Englishman, Thomas Bell. The *Morson* was taken into Philadelphia, where Greenwood remained until April 1783 when peace with France and the former American colonies was agreed. He returned to Lancaster and then had two or three voyages as chief mate in the *Britannia*, as usual to and from the West Indies.

In 1785 Captain Greenwood was given command of the *Molly*. He made several voyages in her to the West Indies up to the year 1789. The owner was a John Jackson, who seems to have been a somewhat dubious character and rather unusually sometimes took ship with Captain Greenwood. Even more unusually, Mrs Jackson sometimes would come along as well. In October 1785, while in Demerara, Greenwood caught yellow fever and Mr Jackson wanted to leave him behind. Too weak to walk, the captain was carried on to the ship by others and recovered on the voyage back to England. Shortly before arriving back at Glasson, they were pursued by a Revenue cutter, as apparently Jackson was a known smuggler! Luckily they escaped. Another trip to Demerara and St Martin's followed and he arrived back off Sunderland Point on 31 January 1787, '... on coming to town, broke all my fine china, my brother Isaac having tied it behind the chaise.'[2] Shortly after this, Thomas Greenwood married Mary Hinde, the daughter of Captain Luke Hinde, a member of a very well-known Lancaster and local seafaring and slaving family.

After one trip in the very small, twenty-ton *Mary*, which arrived at Glasson in August 1790, Thomas Greenwood took over the *Chatsworth*, which belonged to the Lancaster merchants Burrow and Mason and in which he himself had a part share. Over the next three years, while the world was still at peace, he took her four times to the Dutch West Indian island of St Eustasia.

In 1793 Captain Greenwood was given command of what may have been his favourite ship. This was the brand-new, two-decked, three-masted *Aurora*, built by Brockbanks at Lancaster and owned by Burrow and Mason and registered in September of that year. Altogether he made eleven trips to the West Indies in the *Aurora*, during which times he experienced some of the most exciting and dangerous events of his seafaring life.

His first trip in 1793, which coincided with the outbreak of the war with France, was uneventful except that on arrival at St Kitts in the summer of

A
LIST
OF THE
SIGNALS,
FOR EACH VESSEL
BELONGING
THE PORT OF LANCASTER.

Each Vessel's Name arranged in alphabetical Order.

LANCASTER;
Printed by C. CLARK,
1800.

10

Ship SATISFACTION,
A St. George's Ensign at main top-gallant-mast-head, a blue Vergee on the fore top-gallant-stay, and a French Ensign at Mizen Peak.

Brig SALLY.
A blue Vergee with a white ball at fore top-gallant-mast-head and Ensign at mizen Peak, fires five Guns at outer Buoy.

Snow SCIPIO,
An Ensign at main, and broad blue pendant at fore top-gallant-mast-head, the Ensign struck at the outer Buoy for five minutes.

Brig SIX SISTERS,
In the Bay, a blue and white Flag at the fore top-gallant-mast-head, and a red Ensign at the main top-gallant-mast-head.

THETIS,
A blue Vergie at fore top-gallant-mast-head.

TYSON,
A yellow Vergee with three black balls, on the fore top-gallant-mast-head, a French Ensign on the main top ditto. Fires five Guns, first two and then three.

Safe arrival and early identification of a ship were always eagerly awaited both by the owners and the families of the crew. The firing of the ship's cannon while still out in the Bay would apparently bring people to the churchyard where, presumably with the aid of a telescope, they would try to put a name to the incoming vessel.

WITH KIND PERMISSION OF LANCASHIRE LIBRARIES

that year he had no fewer than twenty-five men pressed out of the ship onto the frigate *Solebay*. This left only the captain, chief mate, the cook and six apprentices on board, insufficient to run the ship. He managed to obtain six men from another ship and succeeded in getting to St Eustasia and St Martin's. One assumes that at some stage he was able to recruit additional crew to get the ship back to Glasson the following February.

Further trips to and from the West Indies followed, frequently sailing in convoy. These convoys were large, often with more than 100 vessels involved. A typical escort would be a 74-gun battleship and two sloops of war.

By 1795 St Eustasia had been occupied by the French and destinations tended to be the islands of St Kitts and St Thomas. In that year the *Aurora* managed to escape the attentions of *HMS Woolwich*, which was attempting to press some of her crew.

On his sixth voyage in the *Aurora* a cargo of cotton and mahogany was picked up in St Thomas and they joined a convoy of 120 ships escorted by two 74-gun battleships, the *Minotaur* and the *Centaur*. Captain Greenwood was ordered by the Royal Navy commander in charge of the convoy to sail two miles ahead at night with a light for the ships to follow. This he did and was obviously not prepared to stand any disobedience from other vessels: 'I fired into a large transport for going ahead of us and afterwards he [the Commodore] reprimanded the captain, who afterwards attempted to run us down.' One can well believe it!

On 23 August 1796 the *Aurora* was on her seventh voyage, bound for Martinique when:

> We discovered a sail to the northward, standing to the south-east. At eight o'clock she chased us, having set her square-sail and studden-sails. At nine o'clock discovered she was a schooner and came up fast with us; we took in all studden-sails, top-gallant sails and up-courses, and hove to and prepared for action. At ten a.m. she hoisted French colours, got to windward of us, and began engaging us. We returned her fire in the best manner we could, and after three broadsides she bore directly for us and endeavoured to board us on the larboard side, to avoid which we bore away. She then steered across our stern, and run directly on board us on the starboard side before we could again bear away. We with our small arms and pikes prevented them getting on board, though many got on our chains, and one in particular upon our netting. One of our men attempted to run him through with a pike, he perceiving which dropped his cutlass on our deck and threw himself either into the privateer or the sea. They continued their attempts to board for near a quarter of an hour. I perceived one of the French officers ordering them to renew their vain attempt to board, our people being all ready on our deck arranged and under cover of netting to prevent them boarding. The French boarders appeared to have had enough, and did not show any further attempts to board. I then, with the assistance of my men, raised one of our guns, pointed in such a direction as to fire through the enemy's deck to sink her. We fired this, and the enemy immediately sheered off. We gave him

three cheers in that act. We then found that Andrew Battray, able seaman, was killed; John Langley desperately wounded; M. Turner, the mate, four slugs in his arm; Anthony Crowley slightly wounded. It was a little after eleven when the privateer sheered off. We then got the wounded into the cabin, and immediately prepared, as quick as possible, to resist any further attack, but the privateer lay to the windward, appearing much disabled, and we kept before the wind our course under the topsails only, filling more cartridges: the enemy still laying to repairing her damage. Finding the enemy did not follow us, and after repairing our rigging, at one p.m. set all sail again and continued our course. Thus, by God's assistance and our endeavours, we defeated the enemy. The next day, at six a.m., saw a vessel standing right towards us; called all hands to quarter, supposing her to be the privateer or her consort, but she proved to be a brig, and went astern of us without noticing to the southward. Nov. 24, employed in cleaning fire-arms and making more cartridges. Having no surgeon, I acted as such, dressing the wounds with riga balsam, and giving them bark. During the action I felt as if something struck my head. I took my hat off, and found afterwards that a ball had entered about the middle of the crown and come out at the top. Nov. 26, Saturday, pleasant trade wind; at half-past twelve made the land (distant 10 leagues) – Dominica W. and Martinico S.W. 27th, daylight, almost calm; at two afternoon came to an anchor at Martinico. Got the doctor on board for the wounded. Had no passengers this voyage. I suppose the privateer had 14 guns and 70 men.

However, the danger was not yet over. On 5 February 1797, while on the way back to Lancaster, the *Aurora* was sailing in the company of four other ships, three from Lancaster, the *Atlantic*, the *Ceres* and the *Diana*, together with the *Mersey* from Liverpool, when:

> We discovered a brig on our weather quarter bearing down on us ... At ten all hands to quarters. At quarter past ten the brig came down upon the *Diana*. We then up [our] top-gallant sails, down courses, and bore directly upon the *Diana*, intending to board her and assist on the weather side should the privateer board her on the lee side, but before we were sufficiently near the privateer had boarded and left 14 men on board the *Diana* and sheered off.

In a confused action the French privateer then made off and was unsuccessfully chased by both the *Aurora* and the *Diana*. The fourteen Frenchmen, some wounded, on board the *Diana* (plus two pulled from the sea) were made prisoner, but the British ships had not escaped unscathed as the chief mate of the *Aurora* was killed together with two seamen, as was Captain Fox of the *Diana*. The British ships made their way home, where the *Diana* parted company and was taken by the French. On 10 March 1797 the account reads: 'Arrived at Lancaster; sent our prisoners to the depot at Liverpool. We were received with joy at Lancaster.'

Captain Greenwood continued in command of the *Aurora* ('always a good sailor'). He insisted on exercising the crew of the guns and saying prayers on a daily basis, sailing sometimes in convoy, sometimes not. On one occasion he was appointed civilian commodore of the convoy by the Royal Navy captain in charge of the naval escort, a position which Greenwood clearly relished, not hesitating to fire into those ships which disobeyed instructions. It was also a tribute to his professional skill, which had clearly become known among naval officers. Altogether he made eleven voyages in the *Aurora*, always to the West Indies, and seems to have visited many of the different islands there, including Martinique, Antigua, St Bartholomew's, St Thomas and Tortola. There were no more engagements with French privateers, but a number were sighted and chased away by the naval escort. Illness struck his crew from time to time and burials of those who did not recover were recorded. On one occasion there is a reference to mutiny by a seaman named Hindley. Greenwood had him promptly transferred to a Royal Navy ship, where doubtless he was pressed forthwith. It is presumed that he was sufficiently sensible not to try mutiny again.

In 1799 Thomas Greenwood was given a new ship, the *Mars*, built by Brockbanks and belonging to Burrow and Mason, merchants of Lancaster. In 1800 he went to the Swedish West Indian island of St Bartholomew and the Danish island of St Thomas. On the way home two privateers were sighted and *Mars* was shadowed by one for several hours, the Frenchman hovering just out of range of the *Mars'* guns. Later they encountered a gale: 'January 3rd 1801, blowing hard, ship laboured hard, not as snug as the *Aurora* … 16th, come to anchor at the Buoys, blowing hard. 17th, got into dock [at Glasson].'

The final extract from Captain Greenwood's memoirs relates to his third voyage in the *Mars*, between March and September 1801.[3] As usual he joined 'the fleet', that is the convoy, at Cork. He was ordered by the naval escort pilot to 'hoist a pendent' and bring up the rear of the convoy on the starboard side. It is clear that by now Captain Greenwood had acquired an excellent reputation in naval circles as a reliable master who could be trusted to carry out and enforce the instructions of the escort commander and help keep the ships together. The *Mars* was clearly an excellent sailer and from time to time she would give a tow to those of the convoy having difficulty keeping up. As soon

Apprenticeship agreement between James Greenwood (son of Captain Thomas Greenwood) and Messrs Burrow and Mason, West India merchants of Lancaster 1806.

as land was sighted the *Mars* pressed ahead and was the first vessel to arrive in Carlisle Bay, Barbados, on 8 May, after a passage of 38 days. In gratitude for his help in the Atlantic crossing the Navy only impressed one man of his crew, though he lost two more later to the *Venus* and *Diamond* frigates. At Barbados, '… many merchants and captains to view and admire the *Mars*'.

He then moved on to Martinique, St Croix (or Santa Cruz as he always called it) and St Thomas. The *Mars* sailed for home on 29 July, joining a fleet of over 200 ships outside St Thomas two days later. It was carrying nine passengers, a cargo of sugar, rum, cotton, tortoise shells and mahogany. The voyage back was uneventful, save for a collision in which the *Mars* sustained some damage. The naval commander loaned them his carpenter to help carry out repairs. The convoy became dispersed but after dropping his passengers off near Holyhead arrived at Liverpool on 17 September, 'being the first vessel of the fleet'.

Unfortunately, it is here that the published extracts from Greenwood's memoirs end, but from other records it appears that the *Mars* arrived at Lancaster (or Glasson) from Liverpool in November 1801. There followed three voyages in the *Harriet* to and from St Thomas, Berbice and Dominica between 1803 and 1806, and in 1807 in the *Valentine*, which was apparently later captured, although Greenwood was clearly not on board at the time.[4]

In 1809 he was made master of the *Pusey Hall*,[5] another boat launched the previous year from Brockbanks' yard and owned by James Moore & Co. of Gage Street, Lancaster. By now it would seem that Captain Greenwood was much sought after by Lancaster merchants, and indeed Moores wrote to their agents in Jamaica:

> Our new ship, *Pusey Hall*, Captain Greenwood, sailed with the fleet from Cork on 21st ulto for Jamaica. Captain Greenwood whom you will find to be a man of age and experience.[6]

Apparently Greenwood was given a free hand to find a cargo for the return journey and Moores confirmed they would honour any financial commitment he entered into. *Pusey Hall* was back at Cork on 15 August and reached Glasson Dock two weeks later where she discharged her cargo of rum. Whether some problem then arose is not clear, but on 3 October Moores wrote to their agents that Captain Nicholas Carter had taken over command of the *Pusey Hall*.

Of Thomas Greenwood's last voyage we know a great deal because the logbook of his ship, the *William Ashton*, still survives in Lancaster central library. Though not always easy to read (and Captain Greenwood was clearly

SHIP NEWS.
LANCASTER, SEPT. 2.

ENTERED

August 26 —Halcyon, Bragg, from Trinidad and Tortola, with (from Trinidad) 165 hhds 4 brls sugar 10 punchs 3 pipes rum 10 casks molasses 3 casks 6 bags cocoa 20 pces fustic Thorley & Fell, 44 hhds sugar Bradshaws & Winder, 2 do 20 brls do Richard Fisher, 71 do 15 do 3 punchs rum W Ball & co. (from Tortola) 11 bales cotton G Herdman, 22 do D Tyson, 7 do S S & C Turner.

30.—Pusey Hall, T Greenwood, from Jamaica, with 150 tces sugar Executors of James Hargreaves, 55 hhds 20 tces 12 brls do 20 punchs rum Protheroes & Claxton, 30 hhds sugar R Boyle, jun. & co. 83 punchs rum 31½ tons logwood 13½ tons nicaragua wood J Moore & co. 52 bags cotton France, Fletcher & co. 9 punchs rum J T & W Hornby, 9 pipes 10 punchs 4 hhds rum 15 bags ginger J Simpson & co. 13 punchs rum 10 tces coffee J Welch, 13 pipes 22 punchs 10 hhds rum 3 brls sugar 4 tons ebony T Greenwood.

26 —Vulcan, Houlton, from Kirkcudbright, with charcoal.

30.—Peter, Scully, from Chester, with timber.

CLEARED.

29.—Pitt, Hatheruthwaite, Dominica.
30.—Providence, Leeming, Liverpool.

The *Lancaster Gazette* published weekly shipping news giving details of arrivals and departures.

better at commanding a ship than he was at spelling), it is a fascinating record.[7]

The *William Ashton* belonged to Burrow and Nottage (formerly Burrow and Mason) of Lancaster and as with most, if not all of their ships, she had been built by John Brockbank at his yard in Lancaster. The *William Ashton* was built at a cost of £6,230 0s. 10d., was three-masted, displaced 360 tons and apparently carried sixteen nine-pounder guns. She was named after a planter/

merchant named William Ashton, who carried on business on the Isle of St Croix where Burrow and Nottage regularly traded. The ship was launched on 5 April 1810. The next two weeks she spent at what Greenwood describes as 'the old quay', where presumably she was fitted out with masts and rigging. The *William Ashton* left the old quay on 19 April, which happened on a Good Friday, and went down river, arriving in the dock at Glasson on the 22nd. Any remaining fitting-out was then completed (including probably her guns) and provisions and cargo for the voyage were taken aboard. The former included water, rum, bread, floor, oatmeal, peas, cheese, potatoes, butter, fish and meat – including tripe. The cargo was a very general one, the main items being lime, earthenware, cheese, oil, candles and butter. More unusually, there were sixty tons of hewn stone, fifty grind stones, 24,500 firebricks, twenty large

First page of the log-book of the *William Ashton*, 1810.

WITH KIND PERMISSION OF LANCASHIRE LIBRARIES

sugar-boilers and four hand-trucks. There was also seventeen tons of iron bars. There were thirty separate consignors, including Thomas Greenwood himself, but by far the biggest were the owners, Burrow and Nottage. The principal consignees in St Croix were Messrs Ashton Smith.

The log records the pre-voyage preparations. The crew were divided into two watches: the starboard watch under the captain himself and the larboard under the mate, Mr Winfield. Each consisted of thirteen men and two boys. In addition, there was the ship's carpenter and cook. Each crew member was allocated to a gun, three to each gun. Clearly preparations went ahead very quickly because on 3 May 1810 the log records, 'At eleven this forenoon got under way from the Buoy at Glasson off Bronsil [Basil?] Point.'

The pilot was dropped at 4 a.m. the following day and by 4 p.m. on the 5th: 'Anchored off the fort at Cove [Cork].'

The *William Ashton* stayed at Cork for a week, during which time the ship's longboat broke loose and was brought back by the shore boat. The salvage crew of the shore boat had to be grudgingly paid in total 1½ guineas for their trouble. At Cork a Mr May joined as chief mate, plus two seamen, and additional provisions were taken on board, mainly oats.

On 14 May the ship cleared from Cork – not as part of a convoy as she was sufficiently well armed and manned to allow her sail independently as a 'running ship'. The crossing to the West Indies took about six weeks. The weather was mainly good and the wind was favourable. The crew were kept busy, as time and time again the log reads: 'The people employed at ship's duty and all sails set to the best advantage.'

Captain Greenwood kept a full and interesting ship's log and one can almost sense the tension and concern when other ships were sighted:

Saturday, May the 26th, 1810, first of these twenty-four hours strong breezes and flying clouds, but pleasant weather, all sails set.

It sounds an idyllic scene but:

Five p.m., seen a sail on our starboard beam, all hands to quarters and load our guns.

On this occasion it proved a false alarm. Then, on 10 June,

Strange ship in sight at eleven. Spoke. He was American and bound to the Savannah, thirty days out.

12th of June, a sail in sight standing to the westward … all hands employed at ship's duty, the carpenter and some hands coppering the longboat.

And on the 23rd:

Fresh breezes and flying clouds. At four p.m. brought an American schooner too [sic] with one gun and spoke him. He was from Plymouth bound to Surinam.

There had, however, been time for a little relaxation, as we discover on 7 June: 'The captain caught a Dolfin.' On 26 June, however, 'Made the land believing it to be to the island of Antigua. Distance about six leagues.' And the following day: 'At six a.m. made the island of Santa Crux [St Croix], distance about eight leagues.'

Shortly after the *William Ashton* was boarded by a party from a Royal Navy sloop, who:

impressed four of our men, John Brown, James Patten, David Lyon and Alex Muncaster. At half past eleven a.m. the pilot came aboard … came to anchor, hoist the longboat and got all ready for discharging cargo.

The *William Ashton* remained at St Croix for the next month, unloading and loading cargo. At daily intervals the log records: 'All hands employed discharging cargo.'

There is also reference to negroes 'imployed'. These would probably be slaves. Indeed, on one occasion Greenwood actually refers to them as slaves. Although British involvement in trading and shipping of slaves had been abolished three years previously, the institution of slavery in British possessions continued to exist until 1833. In any case, St Croix belonged to Denmark, albeit in the temporary occupation of the British. The slave trade involving Danish colonies was abolished in 1803, though slavery itself not until 1848.

On 1 July there were visitors: 'Mr Ashton came to look at the ship, then some other gentleman' – obviously he was one of the partners in Ashton and Smith and presumably after whom the ship was named. On 8 July a second seaman, John Peter Grant, deserted the ship and the following day there was a further visit from the Navy; as a consequence John Francis was pressed into the schooner *Netley*. Finally, on 16 July William Etherington was taken ashore to hospital. Greenwood had now lost eight of his original crew, which must have been a considerable worry to him. By the end of July all the loading was complete and the crew made up to twenty-four men and boys. They also appear to have shipped three passengers. On 28 July the ship was 'warped out' and at 'eleven p.m. the pilot went on shore and we made all sail'.

The whole of the cargo, although from different sources, was consigned to Burrow and Nottage. It consisted of a large quantity of sugar (565 hogsheads, 17 tierces and 23 barrels), together with 55 bags of cotton, 39 tons of fustic and two boxes of sweetmeats.

The return journey was also made without the benefit of a convoy, and careful precautions against the enemy were taken. On 6 August the log reads:

> Fresh breezes and pleasant. At six a.m. seen a ship on our larboard quarter. At nine a.m. all hands to quarters. Spoke to her, she was the ship *John Bull* of Liverpool from Guadalupe.

On the same day:

> Spoke to an American schooner from Portland, bound for St Thomas. The captain went on bd and bought one barrell of bread.

On Wednesday 22 August the long-anticipated blow came:

> The first of these twenty-four hours, thick weather, and finally, at six p.m., sent down the royal yards and struck the masts and took in the light sails. At ten p.m. set the fore topmast and lower studding-sail. At daylight seen a strange sail on our weather quarter, steering for us. At nine a.m. fired a gun and hoisted our coulars ... called all hands to quarters and got prepared at eight fired a shot and she hoisted the French coulars.

From the letter printed in the *Lancaster Gazette* a little later, Captain continues:

> We made ready as quick as possible, took in studding-sails et cetera, and waited to receive her; found her to be a long, low ship, pierced for twenty guns, of yellow sides and white figurehead but did not appear to have guns in the two bowports. She commenced action with musketry and then her great guns but did not do any very material damage; after this we began and continued engaging her an hour and a little more and through God's assistance and our utmost exertions we beat her off; after the second broadside she wore round with the intent to rake us; we did the same and

passed under her lee, giving her the other broadside; we passed each other on different tacks, twice, still within musket shot, and we must have done him some material damage with our grape shot or he would not have wore round and left us so soon, as he might have perceived what we were. A little after ten, we then lying to, a ship was passing us to windward at which we fired a shot and she came down hoisting Spanish colours; as the privateer was then in site and in the direction she was steering, she would have been taken in half an hour but for our protection. She proved to be the *Gerona* from Liverpool to New York and the captain was very thankful for his escape and kept with us till evening, when he stood to the southward. On examining our damage, we found our fore topmast badly wounded by a large shot but it stood till we got it fished and another made. We had another shot between wind and water, which we secured as well as we could, but we were so leaky as to require pumping every hour, our rigging and sails a good deal cut, principally by musket shot, but providentially not a man or boy hurt; we were only twenty-five in number altogether.[8]

On 23 August the ship's logbook noted:

Moderate breezes and clear weather. At three p.m. lost sight of the privateer … she boar away to the southward.

Repairs to the topmast were put in hand but the alarm still continued:

Strange sails still in sight and following us. We hauled up to the northward … two strange sails in sight, standing to the westward.

Again one of the unknown ships identified herself by hoisting an American flag. She was spoken to and confirmed that she was from Charleston, South Carolina, 28 days out and bound for Liverpool. Over the next three days the carpenter of the *William Ashton* fashioned the new fore topmast, the damaged one was got down and on 27 August a new one hoisted in its place. Two days later they were off Ireland and 'spoke the Kingsail [Kinsale] pilot-boat'. By now the ship was almost home and on 1 September:

at eight tacked ship. Peel Castle E.S.E., Blackcoom N.E. September the 2nd, at half past two received on board the pilot. Four p.m. came to anchor at the northwest buoy. At five fired six guns to answer the ship's name; on the 3rd of September weighed anchor and came up, at twelve entered Glasson Dock. Tuesday, the 4th of September, 1810, unbent sails and sent on shore the guns.

The Greenwood family grave in St John's churchyard, Lancaster. Some of Captain
Greenwood's large family survived until the 1880s and are buried elsewhere.

PHOTOGRAPH: CARNEGIE

As far as we can tell, Thomas Greenwood never went to sea again – at least
not in command of a ship. Records exist of ship arrivals at Lancaster, giving
details of whence sailed and the name of the master, and his name does not
appear again in these lists. Captain Thomas Dawson, who lived in King Street,
Lancaster, took over the *William Ashton*, sailing her at least twice to the West
Indies before her owners sold her to Liverpool. Captain Greenwood's skill and
courage in preserving his ship was rightly recognised by the underwriters of
Lloyds, who in February 1811 presented him with a piece of silver plate, value
100 guineas, suitably inscribed.

Nothing is known of the reasons for Thomas Greenwood's retirement from
the sea. He was, however, now fifty-two or fifty-three years of age and had
had a hard and dangerous life. He probably felt he had taken enough chances
in his career and that to continue was merely tempting fate. He settled down

in Lancaster and in 1812 he joined the local lending library and remained a substantial and well-known citizen of Lancaster until his death in 1832, aged seventy-four. His tomb can still be seen (with difficulty) in St John's churchyard, Lancaster. He is credited with having crossed the Atlantic 105 times.

His will mentions six sons and one daughter, Hannah, with whom he was living at the time of his death in his house in Great John Street or, as he described it in his will, 'in the Friarige'. After leaving the house and contents to his daughter he bequeathed to his son Luke 'the piece of plate or silver vase which was given to me by the gentlemen Underwriters of Lloyds on condition that on receiving it he pays to my son Robert the sum of fifty pounds and requests that the said vase may remain and be handed down as an Heirloom in my family in remembrance of me.'[9]

Luke Greenwood predeceased his father, dying in St Croix in 1830, so a codicil to the will was prepared and the silver vase went to the second son, Robert, a solicitor. The cup still exists and is currently on loan to the National Maritime Museum at Greenwich.

Of Greenwood's best-known vessel, the *William Ashton*, we know that she continued to sail to the West Indies and in 1813 when commanded by Captain Thomas Dawson took part with two Liverpool ships in the capture of the American schooner *Miranda*. The *Miranda* was re-taken by the American privateer *Paul Jones* but was finally taken by *HMS Unicorn* after 'a smart chase'.

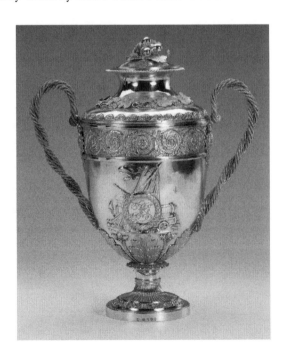

Silver cup awarded to Captain Thomas Greenwood in 1811 by the Lloyd's Underwriters for his successful action the year before.

© NATIONAL MARITIME MUSEUM, GREENWICH, LONDON

CHAPTER SEVEN

Manning the Royal Navy

A S WE HAVE SEEN the transition from the merchant service into the Royal Navy could, for many, be sudden and violent. Although there were rules regarding the impressment of seamen, these were often interpreted rather flexibly, particularly at sea or abroad. Given the circumstances, the sailors taken had little option but to go quietly – once aboard a Navy ship the consequences of disobedience were too terrible to contemplate, and those involved usually accepted the position in which they found themselves while secretly reserving the option to desert when it was safe to do so, which large numbers did.

The Navy of course did have a case. They were the primary agent for the defence of the country and their ships (up to 1,000 in total, requiring at its peak 145,000 men) had to be manned somehow. Unless sufficient volunteers appeared (they never did), then force had to be resorted to man the battleships, the frigates and the many lesser craft which made up the fleet. The obvious source of trained seamen was, of course, the merchant service – an early example occurred in November 1793 when A. and J. Rawlinson's *Active* had many crewmen pressed at Cork.

The Impressment Service, popularly known as the Press Gang, operated ashore, particularly in the major seaports. There is no record of such activities in Lancaster, why is not known, although they were certainly active in Liverpool and Chester. Nine Liverpudlians spent time in Lancaster Castle following an attempt to rescue a number of their fellow citizens from the clutches of the Press Gang, although later receiving a pardon for their crimes.[1]

Men seized at home by the Impressment Service, abroad or on the high seas by Naval captains were in law supposed to be 'seamen', although this description was interpreted somewhat loosely. Nevertheless, the genuine volunteers and the pressed men were together still insufficient in numbers for the fleet, and in 1795 and the following two years a form of conscription was introduced by the prime minister, William Pitt. This was known as 'The Quota', and each county, town, etc. was allocated the responsibility of finding a stipulated number of seamen. The Quota system was not a success because the wrong people were selected. Michael Lewis in his very authoritative *Social History of the Navy* sets out the position very clearly:

> The scheme soon degenerated into a sort of minor gaol-delivery. The counties tended to select their 'bad boys', their vagrants, tramps and idlers. It suited the Justices of the Peace to conclude that the local poacher would be as destructive to French sailors as he was to English birds – and possibly they were right, though there was no shred of evidence to prove it. The town and city authorities sent worse types still – their undesirables; beggars; minor thieves and pickpockets, or people who looked as though they might pick pockets. They even, sometimes, gave the delinquents who appeared before them the alternatives of Quota or Quod.[2]

In 1796 the Quota for Lancaster appears to have been twelve men. How they were selected is not clear but all are described in the returns as 'volunteers' and all received a financial bounty of between £15 and £30, a very substantial sum, although about two-thirds was usually deducted and paid to the county authorities, with the recruit receiving only the balance. This suggests that the recruits were in fact already in gaol and the deductions were made to cover their board and lodging in the Castle. The twelve people constituting Lancaster's Quota Men were a mixed lot, probably regarded by the magistrates as potentially undesirable and if not already in gaol perhaps in receipt of parish relief. The only one from Lancaster itself was Francis Clapham, aged only 16 years, 3 months, and a gardener by occupation. He is described as 5' 3" in height with 'a fresh complexion a little pitted with small pox'. From Gressingham came Robert Toulmin, a 24-year-old labourer, and John Corney, a 19-year-old husbandman from Kellet. Mark Simpson was a smith formerly employed at Halton Forge and William Greenwood had been a skinner at Ingleton. There were also three men from Ireland and one from London, who had clearly found themselves in Lancaster at the wrong time. No doubt the magistrates were happy to have a few non-Lancastrians to make up the numbers. None was taller than 5' 8" and the shortest 5' 1". None of these men appears to have had any seagoing experience, and one can only hazard a guess as to how they made out on board a man of war sailing ship.[3]

The real blame for the hated Press Gang and the inadequate Quota system lay with successive governments who had failed to ensure proper treatment or proper pay for Navy seamen or to introduce a fair system of conscription which applied equally to all classes and conditions. Much has been written about life afloat in Nelson's Navy. The worst horrors were probably more of an exception than the rule, but nevertheless they should not have been allowed to happen.

Since it was a port, albeit a small one, numerous men from Lancaster served in the Royal Navy. With few exceptions not much is known of them apart from their names. Details of their service are hard to find. Midshipman Fayrer, whose family had both Lancaster and Milnthorpe connections, was drowned when his ship, the 74-gun *Defence*, was wrecked in a terrible storm in the North Sea in 1811 and midshipman James Ireland ('son of Mrs Ireland of this town') of the *Dictator 64* was killed by a musket ball during a boat attack on a Danish vessel in the Baltic in October of the same year. Lieutenant John De Vitre, the father of Dr Denis De Vitre, founder of the Royal Albert Hospital and Medical Superintendent at the Lancaster Asylum (later the Moor Hospital), served in the Navy from 1771 onwards. Captured off India by a French frigate in 1782, he was handed over to Hyder Ali, a tyrannical local ruler by whom he was kept in prison for almost two years 'being kept day and night loaded with heavy chains compelled in that state to march from prison to prison under a broiling sun'. Ultimately released, he rejoined the Navy and served until 1798. He died at Lancaster in 1846, an out-pensioner of Greenwich Hospital.[4] The family name is commemorated in De Vitre Street and De Vitre Cottages. John Airey of Lancaster was the sailing master of the 74-gun *Donegal* and was badly wounded in the action off St Domingo in January 1806.

Of more notoriety was Lieutenant William Berry, aged 22 years, a native of Lancaster. On 2 October 1807 he was convicted by a naval court martial of 'the abominable crime of buggery' with a ship's boy. He was hanged on board his ship, the *Hazard*, moored at Plymouth, nineteen days later.

Turning now to seamen, there was Thomas Walmesley who served at the Battle of Camperdown in 1797 aboard *HMS Majestic* and in the 1840s there was living in Lancaster workhouse an old sailor who had been present at Trafalgar, where he had been wounded. Recent research suggests that approximately seventy Lancaster-born seamen fought at Trafalgar, three of whom were actually on board the *Victory* herself on 21 October 1805. Charles Lambert the son of the vicar of Cockerham was also present at the battle. At the age of fifteen years he was serving on board the 100 gun *Royal Sovreign* the flagship of Admiral Lord Collingwood as Volunteer First-Class.[5]

Robert Rigbye, writing under the name of Cross Fleury, in his printed journal for 1904/6 reproduces extracts from a series of letters apparently written between 1806 and early 1811 by one Thomas William Harrison to his mother in Lancaster.[6] During most of this time Thomas Harrison was a seaman in the Royal Navy, firstly in the 44-gun frigate *Anson* and later another frigate, *La Sybille*. He came from a Lancaster family and according to Navy records was probably born in 1784. His father, also called Thomas Harrison, worked with John Brockbank at the latter's shipyard in Lancaster but later vanished at sea. His mother, Ellen Harrison, lived in Wood Street, Lancaster, and he had a brother and sister who also lived in the town.

Thomas Harrison's first letter is written from Cork in 1806. It is not entirely clear, but at this stage it seems that he is still serving on one of the Lancaster West Indian ships but unfortunately he does not mention the name. He ends this letter:

> You may make yourself assured I am in no danger of being pressed. Our captain and all the officers aboard are very kind … both the captain and Mr Warbrick are like fathers to me and all my shipmates are good ones.

The next two letters are both written from *HMS Anson*, into which he had probably been pressed, although the ship's muster roll does not confirm this. The *Anson* had recently taken part in the capture of the Dutch colony of Curacoa, as well as the capture of a Spanish frigate off Cuba but was now part of the Navy squadron taking part in the blockade of the important French naval base of Brest. This blockade of the main French ports was the cornerstone of Admiralty policy throughout most of the war and is generally regarded as one of the supreme naval achievements of all time.

In the first of two letters dated 3 October 1807, at Falmouth, Harrison writes:

> Our unexpected sailing from Plymouth prevented me from getting you my half pay … we have had very bad weather since we sailed from Plymouth. We are stationed off Brest and come to anchor every time the wind is off-shore. We lie so nigh the French squadron that we can discern the men on board … we have a very good old captain who has got us nine live bullocks for our ship's use … The captain has taken a great liking to me and has made me coxwain of the Black Cutter.

The next letter is dated 'Off Brest Oct. 29 1807' and the first part is worth repeating in full as it sheds remarkable light on the attitude of some contemporary Naval officers to their men – an attitude which most commanding officers in any of the services would replicate today on receipt of a letter from an anxious mother:

My dear Mother,

No pen can describe the happy state of my mind when the captain sent for me into his cabin and gave me the letter which you sent to him. He gave me a severe reprimand about being negligent in writing to my parents, but, my dear mother, you know that my affection for you and my dear sister is such that neither time, nor yet distance that lies between us, can ever change it. I wrote you one letter the day that we sailed from Plymouth and sent it to the Post Office by one of the pylots. We were out cruising off Brest for 5 weeks, and had very bad weather. We lost our main topmast and our mizen gallenmast, but we came to anchor off Brest, where we are now lying, and soon got all to rights again … We can see the French fleet very distinctly. There are nine sail of the line, besides frigates and other craft at anchor under the forts, which are very strong. The place is well fortified. Here are 9 sail of the line of us, three of them 3 deckers, besides 2 frigates and some smaller craft. If they would come out we would give them a pretty warm reception. We were in Falmouth a few days ago, and I posted your letter from there, on the 3rd of Oct., which I hope you received. The letter which you wrote to the captain I received off Brest, &c., &c. – Your ever true and dutyfull son.

In December of that year the *Anson* was wrecked in Mounts Bay, Cornwall, with heavy loss of life. The last muster roll of the ship indicates the lucky ones with the word 'survived'. Unlike Thomas Harrison, 'Good old Captain Lydiate' is not among them.[7]

In April 1808 Harrison wrote to his mother again, followed by a longer letter in June of that year from Cork. By this time he is serving on the frigate *La Sybille*. He mentions that he has heard of rioting in England, in particular in Manchester and Bolton, and says 'what can poor labouring people do when they have no work?' He goes on:

The captain was heard to say it would be peace in 3 months and I pray God that I once more have the pleasure of your dear company for I long to have a walk in the Ladies' Walk with some of the pretty Lancaster girls.[8]

He then refers to visiting the frigate *Druid*, where he met two fellow Lancastrians, quite possibly William McKinnel and William Hetton. The latter was captain of the forecastle and discharged on health grounds in 1810. Both these men he says had been pressed out of the *Neptune* but were 'well and hearty'. He goes on: 'They have not got such officers as we have. No men could be better used than we if the whole of the ships in HM's navy were looked through. Half our men are now on shore on leave.'

In February 1809 Thomas Harrison was still serving on board *La Sybille* at Plymouth and recorded the arrival of a large fleet of transports from Corunna – undoubtedly the ships carrying home the army of Sir Thomas Moore driven from northern Spain by the French. He again pays tribute to the captain for 'good useage' and says that they expect to go to Falmouth shortly and escort a convoy to the West Indies. Finally he writes rather sadly, 'I have written three letters to Jane Hebblethwaite since I received any and can get no answer.'

By now Thomas Harrison had been away from home for over three years and had been promoted to able seaman and a letter from his mother brings some not unexpected news about Jane (or Jenny) Hebblethwaite. He replied: 'I find in your letter what I expected to hear some time ago, about Jenny going to be married. I thought some of these strong winds would blow her from her anchor, for I wrote three letters and never got any answer.'

The last letter, also from Cork, is dated 11 April 1811, and in it Harrison mentions that they have recently returned from a nine-week cruise. He seems to have given up all thoughts of peace which occurred quite frequently in earlier correspondence but towards the end he says to his mother: 'You tell me that you have promised [me] to so many young women but I think I can find one in Lancaster yet whom the soldiers have not spoiled. Stop till I get on the Ladies' Walk on a Sunday, I will make some of them look out.'

Almost nothing is known of Thomas Harrison's later life. He did survive the war, unlike his fellow townsman and crewman William Burgess, who was washed overboard and drowned. He subsequently married and had two daughters, both of whom married in their turn. It seems likely that one of them was the custodian of the letters written by her father and made them available to Cross Fleury, who obviously knew the family, who were by then living in Preston.

CHAPTER EIGHT

The soldiers

Over the hills and over the main
To Flanders Portugal and Spain
King George commands and we'll obey
Over the hills and far away

F ROM 1793 until the end of the war the military forces of the country
were, broadly speaking, organised on three different levels. First, there
was the regular army, comprising almost one hundred regiments of the line
plus the Guards regiments and the artillery, together with about twenty-five
regiments of cavalry. All were volunteers, some rather unwilling. The various
regiments, most of which had two (sometimes three) battalions, were known
by numbers and usually had no territorial connection whatever. For example,
the 4th Foot (a most distinguished regiment), which ultimately became the
King's Own Royal Lancaster Regiment, had in fact no connection with
Lancaster itself until the second half of the nineteenth century. However,
the 47th Foot became known as the Lancashire Regiment from a very early
date and certainly had people from Lancaster on its rolls. By 1809 the total
strength of the regular army was over 260,000 men – scattered literally all
over the world, from the West Indies to Australia and from India to Canada,
as the above contemporary song implies. The largest single component of the
army was the field army under Wellington in the Spanish Peninsular, which
by 1813 had increased to almost 50,000 men.[1] A large part of the military
was also retained at home against the dwindling (after 1805) possibility of a
French invasion and of course for internal security. In view of its recent history
more regular troops were allocated to Ireland, from which unhappy country
a sizeable minority of the men of the regular army actually came. However,
there were probably financial and logistic constraints on a higher proportion
of the army serving abroad for any length of time.

Apart from the regular army, the second line of defence was that traditional force, the county militia. Each county had at least one such regiment – Lancashire had three, including the First Royal Lancashire Militia based in Lancaster, with its headquarters in New Street. In theory the militia consisted of men raised by ballot, which was a crude form of conscription. However, in practice most of the more affluent people obtained exemption by paying a fine or hiring a substitute to act in their place. Groups of men would club together and subscribe for this purpose, as indeed did David Cragg in the 1790s – fortunately for him as his name did come out of the ballot! Sadly, the militia muster rolls give no indication from where in the county each soldier came, but clearly there must have been some from north Lancashire, and this is borne out by other records which give details of poor relief paid to the wives of militiamen in and about Lancaster.[2]

The militia were required to serve anywhere in Great Britain, including Ireland, where many units were always stationed. It was comparatively well trained and was used to control civil disorder as well as the invasion threat. Very importantly, it was also widely used as a source for new recruits for the regular army, where ex-militiamen were welcomed as being used to military life as well as being already trained. Militia officers tended to be minor landed gentry or the sons of substantial citizens – like the son of Richard Atkinson of Castle Park, Lancaster, who was a captain in the 1st Royal Lancashire Militia. At least two officers who volunteered for the regular army from the same regiment were killed in the later stages of the Peninsular War.

The third tier of defence consisted of the local Volunteers, who later in the war developed into the Local Militia. The idea of an armed volunteer movement was novel – and it developed on a scale which nobody anticipated. Ultimately over 400,000 men were involved. The larger towns and cities had several volunteer units – Preston had two, each with different political allegiances! Lancaster inevitably became involved and it seems appropriate to look in a little more detail at the raising, in 1797, of the Loyal Lancaster Volunteers.[3]

The Volunteers and the Local Militia

The year 1797 was very bad for Britain and her allies, with General Bonaparte (as he still was) triumphant over the Austrians in Italy. Ireland was in a state of civil war, with French landings in that country and briefly in Wales. The Bank of England suspended payments in gold and last but not least there were extensive naval mutinies at Portsmouth and in the Thames. Locally it was the worst year ever for ship losses to hostile privateers. With all these calamities

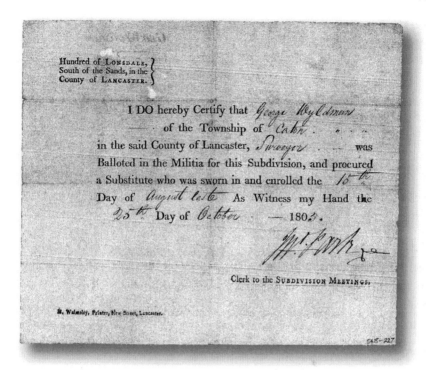

Hundred of LONSDALE,
South of the Sands, in the
County of LANCASTER.

I DO hereby Certify that *George Wyldman*
———— of the Township of *Caton*
in the said County of Lancaster, *Surveyor* was
Balloted in the Militia for this Subdivision, and procured
a Substitute who was sworn in and enrolled the *15th*
Day of *August last* As Witness my Hand the
25th Day of *October* —— 180*3*.

Clerk to the SUBDIVISION MEETINGS.

M. Walmsley, Printer, New Street, Lancaster.

Most men of any substance (unless already an officer) would either pay a fine or hire a substitute to avoid service if balloted to join the Militia. Membership of the Volunteers also gave exemption.

WITH KIND PERMISSION OF LANCASHIRE LIBRARIES

it became clear that a full-scale invasion of the country by the French had now become a very real possibility.

On 27 February 1797, with the mayor, Dr David Campbell, in the chair, a 'numerous and respectable meeting was held of the Gentlemen, Merchants and Inhabitants of the Town to take into consideration the propriety of forming a Volunteer Corps'. This was agreed to unanimously and a committee was quickly formed, with Charles Gibson, a major local figure of Quernmore Park near Caton, as chairman to put matters into effect. It was decided that the volunteers should provide their own uniforms, arms and accoutrements, though if not enough people came forward on these terms the committee would pay for them. It was further agreed that numbers would be limited to 150 men, and that all would serve without pay. Drill evenings would take place twice weekly and a general muster or field day monthly. In no circumstances would the whole or part of the Volunteer Unit go more than a moderate day's march from Lancaster.

A number of formalities had to be completed, such as approval by the War Department (the Earl of Derby as Lord Lieutenant of the county was very helpful here), the appointment of a military agent in London and the recruitment of two or three paid drill sergeants to teach the men their drill. All these caused problems but were overcome in the end. The choosing of an appropriate uniform was of course enjoyable, and the Volunteers must have looked very smart in their 'Scarlett Jacket faced with blue and edged with white Cassimere and Yellow Buttons with L.L.V. and a Crown over the cypher'. With the above went white breeches and waistcoat, white stockings, black cloth half gaiters and black stocks. The headgear was a helmet cap decorated with a white, red or green feather depending whether the wearer was in the Grenadier, Battalion or Light Company. All ranks were to appear on parade with their hair dressed with powder (flour), in imitation of the regular army. The uniforms were manufactured locally – mainly by members of the Volunteers who were in the clothing trade.

The composition of the Volunteers is interesting. Understandably, Charles Gibson was elected as commanding officer, assisted by members of the Bradshaw family (of Halton, presumably), the Worswick family – bankers and merchants of Lancaster – and others. The rank and file were eminently respectable, safe and mainly soundly middle-class. There could be no question of putting arms in the hands of potentially unreliable people. As a consequence the Grenadier Company of fifty men contained ten persons described as merchants, a solicitor, a brewer, a coachbuilder, a customs officer and Alexander Stevens, one of the architects working on the canal aqueduct over the River Lune. In the Light Company among others there were six more merchants, two hatters, two doctors, two coopers, two ironmongers, a rope-maker, a sail-maker and a member of the well-known Gillow family. The Battalion Company had another five merchants (one cannot help feeling that the description 'merchant' was used somewhat flexibly), four lawyers and two cabinetmakers. Most of these were serving as privates. The chaplain was Rev. John Widditt, who was also headmaster of the grammar school. The Volunteers would assemble in Market Square, outside the Town Hall, before marching up to the Greaves to carry out their drill. In their scarlet jackets they would have become a familiar sight to the townspeople. The latter would also have come to enjoy the musical efforts of the drums and fifes, soon supplemented by the band which was formed and which, in contrast to the rest of the unit, received pay. Inevitably some of the initial enthusiasm began to wane and the minutes of the committee refer repeatedly to bad attendance not only by other ranks but by some of the officers as well. The only sanction

TO THE

INHABITANTS

OF THE

TOWN AND NEIGHBOURHOOD

OF

LANCASTER.

THE COMMITTEE for Raising and Equipping the *Lancaster Volunteers,* judging from the nature of the Service in which this Corps is likely to be engaged, consider it indispensibly necessary to provide WARM CLOATHING, as essential to their Health; and the Fund being inadequate to such an additional Charge, they are under the necessity of appealing to the liberality of the Public, for their aid in accomplishing this object.

It will be seen from the following Estimate of the Expence, that a considerable Sum will be required; and when it is known that the object is no less than the preservation of the Lives of a Body of Men, who have Voluntarily stood forward in the DEFENCE of a CAUSE, in which they are only interested in COMMON with OTHERS: the COMMITTEE can entertain no doubt of receiving that Assistance, without which, it will not be in their power to carry this Plan into Effect.

CONTRIBUTIONS in Money, or any of the Articles subjoined, will be thankfully received by Mr. THOMAS WOODS.

Flannel Under-dress,
Cap,
One Pair Woollen Stockings,
And one Pair Strong Shoes, will Cost about £1 4 0 for each
Person, or £463 for the whole.

LANCASTER, 16th NOVEMBER, 1803.

H. Walmsley, Printer, New-Street, Lancaster.

Appeal raised on behalf of the Volunteers raised in 1803.

KING'S OWN ROYAL REGIMENT MUSEUM, LANCASTER

open to those in command was to fine the culprits or arrange a court martial – and the only sanction available to the latter was dismissal from the corps. One of the worst offenders was Jackson Mason, a local solicitor originally an officer but now a private in the Battalion Company. Apparently he 'continually neglected to attend Parade agreeable to the Rules and Regulations of the said Corps whereby he has incurred divers fines to the amount of three pounds or upwards which he refused to pay'. A court martial was ordered (which Mason did not attend), the charge was found to be proved and he was expelled from the corps and judged to be incapable of serving in it again. It might have been expected that such irresponsibility would have resulted in some sort of social sanction or ostracism being applied by his fellow townspeople, but Jackson went on to being mayor in 1804 before dying in 1809 at the early age of 56.

The financing of the Volunteers is not entirely clear. Initially many of the leading citizens of Lancaster had made subscriptions in order to set up the unit and this had been supplemented by later donations together with fines for non-attendance. In addition, the government was supposed to help by paying for the drill sergeants, the fifes and drums and towards the procurement of arms and ammunition – 159 muskets, 4,770 ball cartridges (i.e. 30 rounds per man), gunpowder and 9 pikes for the non-commissioned officers. The arms and ammunition were kept in the castle. Certainly those who could, probably the majority, were expected to make a financial contribution to their own equipment. Not surprisingly it proved difficult to get the money from the government, although it seems to have been achieved in the end, though not before the London military agent, Mr Russell, had been dismissed for 'neglect of duty' and a Mr Hemans appointed in his place.

In April, 1798 the Volunteers received by way of gift two pieces of artillery. They came from Dr Wilson, the brother of the squire of Dallam Tower at Milnthorpe, who himself had a house in Church Street, Lancaster. As a consequence a small gunnery section was formed, consisting of two officers, four NCOs and twelve men. They wore the traditional Royal Artillery blue jackets with black belts, with the remainder of their uniform as the Infantry. They must have made a brave sight with their guns rattling over the cobblestones of Lancaster.

By 1799 the urgency had gone out of the situation; major naval victories against the Dutch, the Spanish and the French were supplemented by striking, if short-lived successes, on land by the Austrians and Russians. All these, together with the crushing of the rebellion in Ireland, made the likelihood of invasion much less and as a consequence the Volunteers began to parade only once fortnightly and a number of the officers resigned. Nevertheless, the corps continued in being and payment was now being made not only to the band but also to those men who had not paid for their own uniform and equipment – in other words, the poorer members of the unit. Throughout this difficult period Charles Gibson still attended just about every meeting and parade and set an example of conscientious service not always followed by his fellow officers. When the regiment was finally stood down at the Peace of Amiens in 1802 he was presented with a silver cup by all ranks as 'a mark of their esteem'. He certainly deserved it.

The final meeting of the Volunteer Committee took place on 3 May 1802, when it was agreed that each Volunteer would be paid £2 2s. 0d. for his arms and accoutrements 'to be deposited pursuant to the orders of the Government', and that the two pieces of artillery should be returned to Daniel Wilson (if permitted by the government) 'with the thanks of the Corps'. It was further agreed that the uniforms and headgear should be retained by their wearers and that any surplus monies (£352 12s. 0d. in Worswick's Bank) should be disposed of as the principal officers thought fit. The final decision was that the mayor and officers of the Corporation be asked to take charge of the 'Records, Regulations, Colours and Musical Instruments and other property of the Loyal Lancaster Volunteers'.

The last parade was on the 12 May 1802, and at a ceremony on the open ground behind the Castle a royal salute was fired by the artillery and the colours were carried into the churchyard from whence they were taken into the church and laid on the Communion table. The whole regiment then marched to Market Square, where they were formally disembodied before 'partaking of an entertainment' at the Town Hall. And that was that – or so they thought.

In the meantime, the First Royal Lancaster Militia also returned to Lancaster to be disbanded after eight years' service in various parts of the country. A week after their arrival in the town, on 24 April, the *Lancaster Gazette* reported:

On Saturday last the First Royal Lancaster Militia commanded by Colonel Stanley was disembodied in this town. The regiment was mustered at 5 o'clock in the morning when the thanks of the two Houses of Parliament were read to the men, after which they were all settled with (having previously examined their separate accounts the day before). The greatest order prevailed throughout the day and before night nearly the whole of them had left town for their respective homes.

Two fine medallions struck in 1802 and 1805 on behalf of Daniel Eccleston a well-
known, if slightly eccentric, Lancastrian. The reverse of the Bonaparte medallion
(struck in a mood of optimism at the time of the short lived Peace of Amiens) describes
the French Emperor as one who 'gave Liberty to France and Peace to the World'. The
inscription on the George Washington medallion is less provocative! Eccleston sent a
copy to the contemporary President of the USA and received a suitable letter of thanks.

PHOTOGRAPHS: CARNEGIE

The summer of 1802 was, ostensibly at least, a time of celebration. There was
general rejoicing at the return of peace and anticipated plenty. Bryant mentions
a cartoon showing John Bull making merry with long-absent friends – Old
Stout, Best Wheaten Bread, Excellent Fresh Butter, Prime Hops and Jamaican
Rum.[4] Even in Lancaster there was a spirit of optimism, with the local harvest
being described as the best ever and high wages being paid. True, the years
1801 and 1802 were bad for West Indian trade and fewer ships had arrived from
those islands than had been the case for many years. Doubtless this was felt to
be a temporary aberration. In the meantime the town's two shipyards were still
building; a new cotton mill (the first of any size in Lancaster) opened in 1802 at
White Cross; and those other industries associated with or dependent upon the
West Indian trade, such as George Crosfield's sugar refinery business in Sugar
House Alley and Dilworth and Dockray's rope works, still flourished, together
with sail making, sailcloth making and furniture establishments. The annual
parade of the friendly societies, which took place each spring, maintained its
numbers (indicative to some extent of the state of trade) and the first census
of 1801 showed comparatively few people unemployed. In July 1802 a general
election took place; it appears to have been particularly disorderly, with some
personal injury and a considerable number of broken windows.

However, the international situation, in particular relations with France, deteriorated during the late autumn of 1802 and by March the following year had reached crisis point. To what extent the majority of the townspeople read the *Lancaster Gazette* is not clear, but undoubtedly the more literate did. Although a poor newspaper in many ways, it did give a lot of space (culled from the London papers) to national and indeed international affairs and this information would be spread widely by word of mouth. As a consequence, the announcement in March that the Militia were to be called out and the Navy increased and put on standby must have sent the clearest possible message that hostilities were likely to be renewed – as indeed they were in May of that year.

As we have seen, hostilities at sea were commenced almost immediately and in this connection it was fairly clear that the country would be able to hold its own, particularly in safeguarding its enormous overseas trade (notwithstanding the French privateers) and in maintaining a blockade of the French naval ports. However, in 1803 Napoleon had no continental enemies and was able to divert all his attention to crushing Great Britain. As a consequence, in the summer of 1803 the French army began to concentrate at Boulogne and a massive construction programme of landing ships was begun. Clearly invasion was once again a real possibility.

By now any lingering sympathy for the French Revolution had largely vanished and Napoleon Bonaparte could now be seen for what he was – an

The calling out of the Militia was one of the first signs that war with France was to be renewed in the spring of 1803.

WITH KIND PERMISSION OF
LANCASHIRE LIBRARIES

LANCASHIRE MILITIA.

HIS Majesty, by his Warrant under his Sign Manual, having ordered the Lord Lieutenant of this county to draw out and embody the Militia of the county of Lancaster, with all speed; His Lordship hath appointed all the Militia-men of this county, to assemble on MONDAY the fourth day of April next, as follows.:

The First R. L. M. at Lancaster.
The Second R. L. M. at Liverpool; and
The Third R. L. M. at Preston.

And all Officers, Non-commissioned Officers, and all Militia-men and others, whom it may concern, are hereby required to take NOTICE, and give their attendance accordingly.

By order of the Lord Lieutenant of Lancashire,
THOMAS WILSON,
Clerk of the General Meeting of Lieutenancy.
PRESTON, MARCH 18, 1803.

exceptionally able, violently ambitious and totally unscrupulous person whose object was the subjugation of Europe to the will of France or, more accurately, to himself.

The First Royal Lancashire Militia re-formed at Lancaster on 4 April and some six weeks later, on 20 May, left Lancaster for Chelmsford. The Second RLM from Liverpool and the Third RLM from Preston followed a few days later. Everywhere the roads of England were full of marching men – the Cumberland Militia passed through Lancaster *en route* for Liverpool and Ireland, the Westmorland for Sunderland and the Royal Cheshire for Norwich. Obviously, the greatest threat from France lay on the south and south-east coasts and the regular army and militia were concentrated in those areas. Indeed, the tents of the French army were plainly visible in the hills

To the INHABITANTS of the Hundred of LONSDALE, SOUTH of the SANDS.

IT having been resolved, by the Lord Lieutenant, and a most numerous and respectable Meeting of the Lieutenancy, of this county, held at Wigan, the 27th instant, that the Lieutenants of Divisions should recommend, in their respective Districts, PUBLIC MEETINGS, for the purpose of promoting VOLUNTEER CORPS, for the General Defence of the Kingdom, in case of Invasion; I therefore, in pursuance thereof, do request a MEETING of the INHABITANTS of THIS DISTRICT, on MONDAY next, the 1st day of August, at the CASTLE of LANCASTER, at eleven o'clock in the forenoon; and I cannot forbear expressing my confidence, that the same spirit of loyalty and attachment to our King and Country. the same zeal for the protection of our families and properties, against the attempts of a rapacious and insolent enemy, which are so conspicuous in every other part of the kingdom, will be found equally to prevail here: And, I trust, the appearance and resolutions of that Meeting will shew, that the exertions of this part of the district, over which his Majesty has been pleased to place me, will not be inferior to any, in support of our glorious Constitution, and of every blessing we enjoy, as Englishmen. CHARLES GIBSON, Lieutenant of Division.

Quernmoor-Park, July 28, 1803.

Call to Arms. This led to the formation of the Volunteers in 1803.

above Boulogne where they could be viewed with the help of a telescope by the apprehensive or the merely curious walking on the cliffs on the other side of the Channel.

All these events made it almost inevitable that there would again be a place for a volunteer movement and this proved to be the case on a much larger scale than in 1797. Hundreds of units were formed all over the country 'to meet a formidable, proud and tyrannical foe'; Lancaster was no exception.[5] Starting in mid-July there was a series of public meetings, the prime movers in which were Charles Gibson, newly appointed Lieutenant of Division, Thomas Shepherd, the mayor of Lancaster, and the very well-known, highly regarded and articulate Dr David Campbell. The latter made a powerful and intelligent speech pointing out that a successful invasion on this occasion would not merely involve a change of monarch (as was the aim of previous attempts in the early part of the eighteenth century) or the benefit of one section of the community over the other but would involve the destruction of 'our arsenals, our towns, our manufactories; of everything which can prove an obstacle to the ambition or rising trade of France'. He went on: 'The troops to be employed are enticed to this adventure by the allurement of the plunder of the country to be laid waste.'

Due to his new position as Lieutenant of the Division of North and South Lonsdale Charles Gibson was unable to take command of the new Volunteers, so this position went to his former deputy, John Bradshaw of Halton. Few, if any, records survive relating to the re-forming of the Volunteer Corps in 1803, although some information is available from the pages of the *Lancaster Gazette*. Certainly the new Volunteers were much more numerous on this occasion and initially there were six companies of infantry comprising sixty men in each and, in view of these increased numbers together with the request for subscriptions for the purchase of warm clothing, it seems likely that the social mix was much broader than six years previously. One of the new breed was, perhaps, Sergeant Thomas Ralph, who died in June 1806. He was a plumber and glazier by trade, with premises in Chancery Lane, where he employed two apprentices. Rather touchingly, he was given a funeral at the parish church 'with military honours'. Also in the Volunteers were ten employees from Brockbanks' shipyard. By 1804 the *Gazette* reported numbers to be 900, representing a large increase accounted for in part perhaps by the inclusion of men from Caton, Halton, Warton and Skerton and other outlying areas. While the threat from France continued everyone worked with a will, notwithstanding the lack of leadership and incompetence displayed by the government.[6]

By October the Volunteers had appeared in their new uniforms and had received their arms. In September 1803 and 1804 they were reviewed by the Duke of Gloucester and his son, Prince William, the former being the commander of the North West Military District based at Liverpool. These visits by members of the royal family (the first since 1745) caused great excitement, and there were undoubtedly spontaneous outbursts of loyalty by the citizens of Lancaster. Included in these tours was a review of the Volunteers in Dalton Square, a visit to the theatre in St Leonardsgate, a trip to Clougha Pike and finally to the debtors' part of the prison in the Castle. The debtors assured their royal visitors of 'their attachment to the cause of their King and Country against the arrogance and threat of an implacable enemy'. They also pointed out that, due to their present position, they were currently unable to take a more active part in the defence of the nation.

The training and appearance of the Volunteers clearly improved and they were the subject of satisfactory reports from the government-appointed

How Lancaster people read about the victory of Trafalgar – and the death of Nelson.

WITH KIND PERMISSION OF LANCASHIRE LIBRARIES

NAVAL VICTORY.

We have on this day to announce to our readers, the most GLORIOUS, the most DECISIVE VICTORY ever obtained by the NAVY of GREAT BRITAIN; but we have at the same time to communicate an event, the knowledge of which will fill every British bosom with the deepest anguish—the GREAT, the GALLANT NELSON is NO MORE!!—*See our London news.*

The above important news was brought to this town by a private gentleman late on Thursday evening; but the melancholy intelligence of the death of Lord Nelson was not received till the mail arrived, about eleven o'clock yesterday morning, when, paradoxical as it may appear, joy appeared in every countenance, shaded by melancholy; for never was the death of a man so much lamented (tho' shrouded in glory) as on this occasion —He was the Nation's Hope! The memory of him will be imprinted on the mind of Englishmen till time shall be no more. —The GAZETTE ACCOUNT of this MOST GLORIOUS VICTORY is given in our last page.

inspecting officers. Apart from the regular parade days, the corps were sometimes called out for longer periods of permanent duty: in May 1804, spending three weeks at Ormskirk and in the following year a similar length of time was passed in Preston, with Volunteers from Ulverston, Bolton and Preston spending similar time in Lancaster – sometimes travelling by boat on the canal.

The immediate threat of an invasion probably passed in the early autumn of 1805. Napoleon, now emperor of France, had made elaborate plans for his Toulon fleet to escape from the Mediterranean to the West Indies, having drawn off part of the Royal Navy in so doing. It was then to return to Europe and release the large French fleet in Brest (somehow without a battle) and the combined fleet was then to head up the English Channel to escort the invasion flotilla to the shores of Kent and Sussex. Although the first part of the plan worked, the French Navy was unequal to the task and Napoleon waited in vain at Boulogne for his victorious ships to arrive. By the end of August he could delay no longer. By dint of diplomacy and substantial subsidies William Pitt, the prime minister, had set eastern Europe ablaze and the Austrian and Russian armies were preparing to move. On 3 September 1805, the Grande Armée broke camp on the French coast and began an epic march to the Danube. In two months it was all over, with first the Austrians and then the Russians being outmanoeuvred before being totally defeated at the battle of Austerlitz. Three weeks earlier on 21 October, in accordance with Napoleon's orders the French fleet trying to escape from Cadiz to return to the Mediterranean was intercepted by Admiral Nelson and disastrously defeated at Trafalgar.

The French military involvement in eastern Europe (continued against Prussia in 1806 and Russian in 1807) together with the Trafalgar defeat ensured that an invasion of Britain was no longer a viable proposition, although the invasion fleet still remained in being at Boulogne and neighbouring ports as a potential threat to this country. With the benefit of hindsight, the collapse of the invasion plans can be seen more clearly today than it could at the time, and as a consequence the Volunteers remained in being, though perhaps with diminishing enthusiasm. Nevertheless, they continued with their parades, drills and inspections and would also turn out for church parades at St Mary's church and for the annual celebrations for the king's birthday.

In 1808 there was a complete change in official policy, with the formation of a Local Militia – quite separate from the long-established County Militia. Government support was withdrawn from the Volunteers, many of whom transferred *en bloc* into the new force. Between 200 and 300 of the old

Lancaster Volunteers transferred into the Local Militia, encouraged by a very useful bounty of £2 2s. per man and thereafter one shilling a day while embodied plus 1d. daily for beer money. The remaining men were found by ballot, in respect of which substitutes were not allowed. Matters were now on a much more professional basis and military discipline was applied. In June 1810 a private in the Local Militia was publicly flogged on the parade ground behind the Castle for not joining the regiment until the day before the period of training ended. Somehow one cannot see that happening to Jackson Mason. The commanding officer was still John Bradshaw and his officers were substantial citizens such as Thomas Salisbury, John Bond, Stephen Moore – genuine West Indian merchants or members of well-established Lancaster families, including the Horners, Cumpstys, Armstrongs, Higgins and Sewards. The activities of the corps were faithfully reported by the *Lancaster Gazette*. For example, on 18 May 1811:

> On Wednesday last the Lonsdale Regiment of Local Militia commanded
> by Lt Col. Bradshaw were reviewed on Lancaster Moor by Mayor General
> Gower. This fine corps mustered 1,100 strong; their steadiness while going
> through the manual and platoon exercise was highly spoken of and their
> marching and wheeling would have done credit to a veteran regiment ...
> And on Thursday having completed their fourteen days training the regiment
> was disembodied. Their conduct during the whole of the time was such as to
> ensure to them the good wishes of the inhabitants.

The Local Militia remained in being and was embodied every year up to and including 1813. In 1812 it played a part in providing local security for the castle during the Luddite disturbances elsewhere in the county. The war having ended in April 1814, the Local Militia was not called out again, although its band appears to have performed during the peace celebrations of that year.

It is easy but unfair to mock the Volunteers or the Local Militia (or for that matter the Second World War Home Guard) from the comfort and security of the more cynical twenty-first century, but they were not derided at the time. They certainly contributed to the actual as well as the perceived security of the nation and many units would certainly have acquitted themselves well in action had they been put to the test. Motives for joining were, of course, very mixed. Membership of the Volunteers and the Local Militia certainly gave exemption from the ballot for the County Militia but simple patriotism, public opinion and a sense of novelty and adventure also played their part. At

The Local Militia (not to be confused with the Royal Lancashire Militia) were the successors to the Volunteers. They were a more professional body and subject to military discipline.

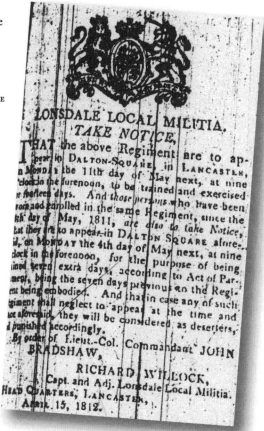

all events those who served would remember the comradeship and good times as well as the hardships for all the rest of their days and there would be an unspoken bond between all those who had been involved.

The County Militia and the Regulars

As far as the County Militia is concerned, we have seen how the First Royal Lancashire Militia were re-formed in the spring of 1803 before moving to the south of the country as part of the anti-invasion force. They remained at various places in the south and south-west of England during the next eight years and while at Weymouth came to the notice of the king and the rest of the royal family due to the excellent state of the regiment and the musical expertise of their band – particularly the drummer, Jack Hayes from Lancaster, who was renowned for his dexterity playing with two sets of drumsticks at the same time. While at Weymouth George III presented the regiment with a pair of silver kettledrums and Queen Charlotte a new set of colours. In 1811 the unit was moved to the East Midlands and then to Hull in response to the rioting in this area before going to southern Scotland and finally to Ireland, where they were stationed when the war ended. There was delay in being disbanded, partly because the regiment was in Ireland and partly because of the resumption of war with France in 1815, culminating in the battle of Waterloo. As a consequence it was not until 2 March 1816 that the *Lancaster Gazette* was able to report:

> On Tuesday last the First Royal Lancashire Militia under the command of Lt Col. Plumbe arrived here from Ireland. They were met at some distance from the town by a great number of people notwithstanding the wetness of the day. The regiment marched from here in 1803 since which we are informed about 1500 have volunteered out of it into the regulars. They are a fine body of men and are expected to be disembodied on Saturday next.

As indeed they were.

It can be confirmed that large numbers did indeed volunteer into the regular regiments of the line. Favourite regiments appear to have been the 95th Rifles, the 34th, the 52nd, the 5th and 7th Foot as well as the Guards regiments. Quite frequently a Militia Officer volunteered and if he brought enough men with him was awarded a commission in the regular army.

Service in the militia was for a minimum of five years and if one had been balloted for duty, it was clearly not popular. A very large proportion of men balloted sought exemption from serving themselves, by paying a statutory fine or paying for a substitute. Substitutes had to serve for the full period that the militia as embodied. Many unemployed men volunteered for the militia for economic reasons. For wives and children left destitute by the absence of the family wage-earner the law allowed the parish to pay a small allowance – unlike the families of the regular soldiers who were not entitled to parish relief. While in being the militia were probably under-employed and were occasionally borrowed by farmers to help with the haymaking or harvest. For the First Royal Lancashire Militia there was the odd excitement, as in June 1807, when the town of Chudleigh in Devon was largely destroyed by fire, the militiamen rendered aid and assistance and lent their tents for shelter. On another occasion, in March 1805, the *Lancaster Gazette* reported:

> A smuggler [vessel] which landed a cargo on this coast [Romney Marsh] a few days since was seized by a Revenue Cutter but the officers, from

the opposition they experienced, could not keep possession of her without the assistance of the military. A party of the First R.L.M. stationed at Dungeness had not been long on this duty when they were attacked by about one hundred smugglers ... a smart engagement ensued.

During the course of the firefight two smugglers were shot and killed and several wounded. Nevertheless, it is possible to understand that many militiamen, particularly those who were single, might opt for the life of a regular soldier and the unknown hazards of campaigning in Spain.

Of Lancaster men serving in the regular army little is known, but it has been possible to glean some information from records held in the National Archives at Kew. These relate to soldiers admitted to pension and as these records are now computerised it is possible fairly readily to research them by reference to a soldier's place of birth.[7] Between 80 and 100 names are revealed of regular soldiers who were apparently born in Lancaster and who served in the war. Other records, admittedly incomplete, give the names and place of birth of soldiers who were in French prisoner of war camps, and regimental casualty returns also sometimes give helpful information. Two who did not survive were John Stirzaker, a carpenter, and Richard Forrest, both from Lancaster and both serving in Spain in the 47th Foot. They died in May 1809 and December 1810, respectively. John Metcalf, also of the 47th Foot, died on 9 October 1813, probably of wounds sustained at the storming of San Sebastien in the summer of that year when his regiment was heavily engaged and suffered grievous losses. Of the same regiment was Corporal John Ratcliffe of Lancaster, who was wounded in the chest in the same action. He recovered and later served in India, where he was wounded again. He was discharged, 'worn out', in 1819 after ten years' service. Thomas Bradley came from Yealand and enlisted in the Coldstream Guards in 1813. He served at Waterloo two years later, where he was wounded in the leg. He was discharged on health grounds while serving in the Army of Occupation in France in 1818. Thomas Clarke came from Lancaster and enlisted in the 7th Foot in 1810 at the age of eighteen. He was a shoemaker by occupation and was wounded in the right arm at Salamanca in the summer of 1812. He was discharged as unfit for further service in the following year. Thomas Clarke's initial pension seems to have been 6d. daily. However, he survived until at least 1864, by which time his daily allowance had been increased to 1s. 2d. Another local man, Private Edward Fox, was in the cavalry, serving no less than twenty-two years in the 1st Royal Dragoons, both in the Peninsular War and at Waterloo. On his discharge in 1827 he went to live in Preston. Sergeant Samuel Nailer served nine years in the 3rd Foot Guards (later the Scots Guards) and was wounded in the stomach in south-west France in 1814 towards the end of the war. He appears to have come from Heysham and was discharged later that year on health grounds. And there were many others from Lancaster and neighbouring districts – Edward Beeston of the 7th Hussars; John Brittlebank of the 20th Light Dragoons who returned to his home town in 1814. Francis Raby, originally a hairdresser from Lancaster, enlisted (probably from the militia) into the Coldstream Guards in 1810. He served in the Peninsular, was wounded in the hand at Fuentes d'Onoro and was present at Waterloo. He was discharged after eleven years' service because of his wound and because of the reduction in size of the army. Private John Dean served for less than two years in the 71st Foot before being discharged by reason of a severe gun shot wound in the thigh sustained near Bayonne in December 1813.

Finally there was William Thornton. He was born in Lancaster and in 1810 when he was eighteen years of age he enlisted in the 1st Life Guards. He was a big man, 6 feet 1 inch tall, with brown hair and grey eyes. As far as can be seen, he did not accompany that part of his regiment which went to Spain, but he certainly fought at Waterloo, where he was heavily engaged. In December 1815 the *Lancaster Gazette* published extracts from a letter written by William Thornton to his mother, who lived in Union Square, Lancaster. He gives a vivid account of being in action on both 17 and 18 June 1815, and makes clear his admiration for his troop commander, Captain Kelly, 'one of the bravest men who ever drew a sword'. The latter exhorted his men just before leading a charge with the words, 'My lads, do not be daunted, follow me and I will lead you to glory.' At the main battle on 18 June the Life Guards were in action again and they took part in 'nine charges against the French', during the last of which Captain Kelly was wounded. Private Thornton escaped unscathed and his letter to his mother was dated 4 November from just outside Paris. He was discharged from the army in 1835 'unfit for further service'. He was described as a good and efficient soldier and 'his ailments [were] not contributed to by intemperance, vice or design'. Apparently, William Thornton's health had suffered from a severe cold and cough caught while on duty at the trial of Queen Caroline in 1820 and by falling down the barracks steps in 1832.

With this short account of the life of William Thornton it is possible to conclude the study of Lancaster's regular soldiers. But there would of course be many others from this city and neighbourhood who fought, suffered and in some cases died in Spain and Portugal, in a French prison camp or on that Belgian battlefield on a June Sunday almost 200 years ago.

Gateway of Lancaster Castle 1802 by Freebairn. Note the stonemasons working under the trees on the left.

General (somewhat idealized) view of Lancaster 1802 by Freebairn.

The recently built aqueduct over the river Lune with horse-drawn barge in transit.
Gideon Yates. Early nineteenth century.

The Old Bridge over the river Lune. The Millennium Bridge now occupies the site.
The Old Bridge became more or less redundant following the completion of Skerton
Bridge in 1788. It was purchased in 1802 by John Brockbank who promptly demolished
the northernmost arch to allow more room for vessels launched from his shipyard. The
remaining three arches collapsed over the years, the last one falling in December 1845.
By Gideon Yates who produced many views of Lancaster in the first ten years of the
nineteenth century.

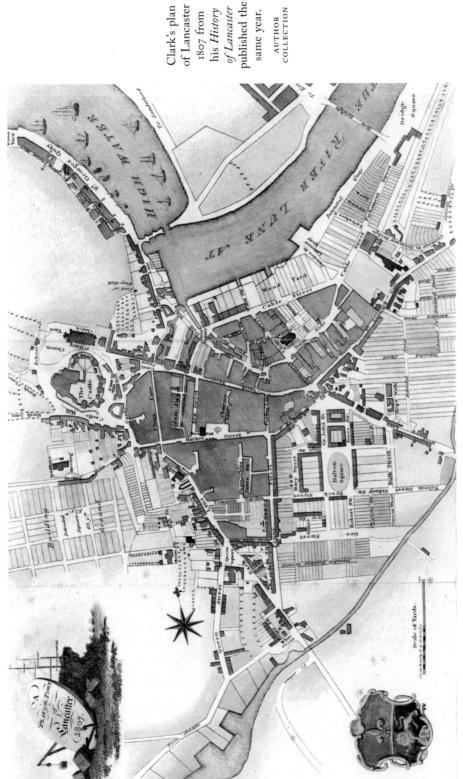

Typical early nineteenth-century merchant ship the *Isabella* by J.W. Carmichael – not alas from Lancaster!

© NATIONAL MARITIME MUSEUM, GREENWICH, LONDON

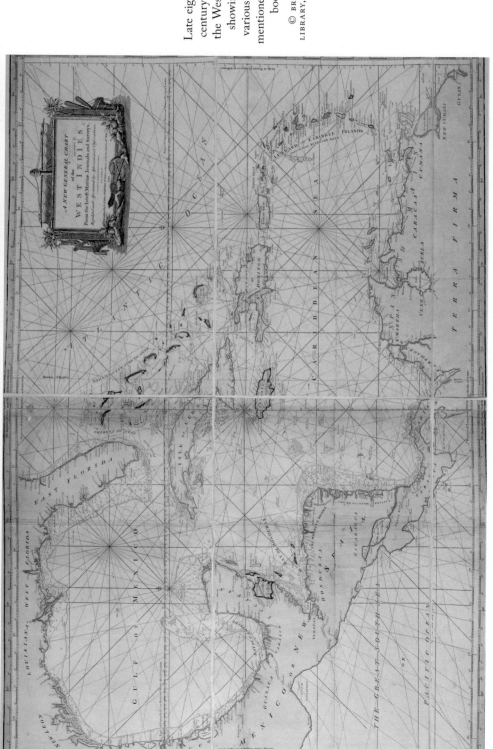

Late eighteenth-century map of the West Indies showing the various islands mentioned in this book.

© BRITISH LIBRARY, LONDON

A scene repeated regularly throughout the war – a privateer returning to port with an enemy prize. Here the privateer (on the left) is probably the *Viper* of Liverpool by J. Parry.

© LIVERPOOL MARITIME MUSEUM

A late eighteenth century Liverpool Slave ship off the coast of West Africa. By William Jackson.

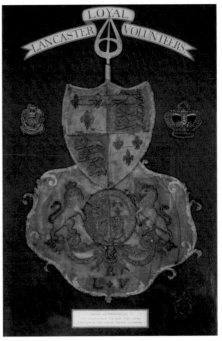

The colours of the Loyal Lancaster
Volunteers.

© KING'S OWN ROYAL REGIMENT MUSEUM

All that remains of the original colours of
the Loyal Lancaster Volunteers.

© KING'S OWN ROYAL REGIMENT MUSEUM

Hannah Smith, executed behind Lancaster
Castle in 1812 for rioting.

© ROBERT POOLE

Silver cup presented to Captain Thomas Wilson for his action in fighting off a French Privateer in 1798. This cup was discovered in a Washington DC antique shop soon after this book was first published.

© ORI BEN CHORIN

The *Abram* built at Brockbank's shipyard 1805/6. Only known picture of a Lancaster built ship. This illustration shows the *Abram* post 1818 in her new guise as a whaler based in Hull. She was wrecked in 1862.
Hull Whaler *Abram*, 1863 (oil on canvas board) by James H. Wheldon (1832–93)

PHOTO © HULL MUSEUMS / BRIDGEMAN IMAGES

The Judges' Lodgings, c.1805 by unknown artist (LANLM.1956.7.42), bequeathed by Miss Heald in 1956. The scene and buildings remain almost unchanged today.

© LANCASTER CITY MUSEUMS

CHAPTER NINE

The politician, the gentleman and the absentee vicar

A s we have already seen, Lancaster was a small place at the end of the eighteenth century. Anyone of any eminence, however slight, would be known to almost everybody in the town – if not by sight then certainly by reputation. If one was active in local affairs, was a major landowner and for a number of years one of the Members of Parliament, he would be instantly recognisable and everyone would have an opinion on him – favourable or unfavourable.

John Fenton Cawthorne

Such a person was John Fenton Cawthorne. He had two houses – Fenton Cawthorne House in Market Street, the current site of the General Post Office, and Wyreside Hall near Dolphinholme. Born John Cawthorne in 1753, he was the grandson and greatgrandson of two successive vicars of Lancaster. His father was a lawyer who became recorder – a junior judge – of Lancaster. His marriage in 1778 was rumoured to have brought him a sizeable dowry of £30,000. His middle name, Fenton, was acquired in 1781 in anticipation of his acquiring his mother's property in Wyresdale, which he did on her death in 1798 although he appears to have managed it before that date. He also acquired the Recordership of Lancaster on his father's death in 1791. He was educated at Queen's College, Oxford, and Gray's Inn where he qualified as a barrister.

Between 1783 and 1796 Cawthorne was MP for Lincoln by reason of the influence of his father-in-law, Lord Delavel – such influence (or 'interest' as it was usually known) being invaluable both to election and subsequent advancement in political life. Once in Parliament Cawthorne transferred his political support to William Pitt, the prime minister, though showing none of the wisdom, judgment and ability of the latter. He supported all the repressive measures against the radicals of the time, was hostile to any fuller measures for religious toleration and, in particular, was totally against the abolition of the slave trade. While an MP, Cawthorne regularly badgered Pitt for favours for himself and his family, but with little success. Outside the House of Commons he became a member of the Westminster Militia, of which he subsequently became Colonel, a move which led to his disgrace. In March 1796 he was court-martialled on numerous charges of financial misconduct.

Right: John Fenton Cawthorne as a young man by Romney.

Below: A plan of 1798 showing the proposed development behind John Fenton Cawthorne's house (marked A) in Market Street. The development did proceed slowly but not as planned. Plot 18 was later given as the site of the Girls' Charity School. The houses erected on plots 19–24 were demolished after World War II to provide parking for postal vehicles. Fenton Cawthorne House itself was demolished in 1921. The front entrance portico was preserved and re-erected at the rear of the Storey Institute on Castle Hill, where it still remains.

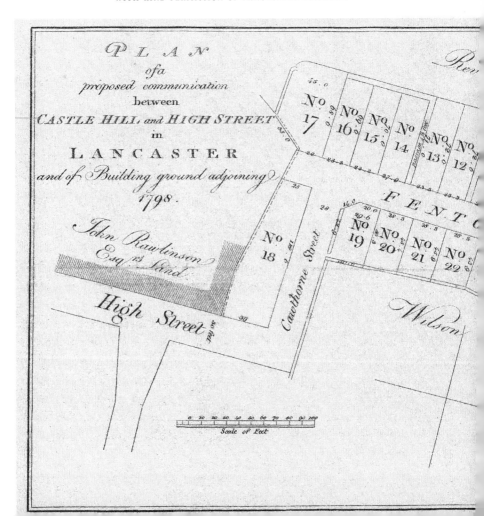

Upon his conviction for fraud and embezzlement he was cashiered from the army for 'conduct unbecoming the character of an officer and gentleman'. His expulsion from the House of Commons followed, with Pitt himself supporting the motion to exclude. By 1797 Cawthorne was reported as being in debt to the tune of £50,000. Notwithstanding his expulsion from the Commons, Cawthorne had his eye on one of the two seats at Lancaster; despite spending what was believed to be the sum of £3,000, his election campaign in 1802 was unsuccessful. Cawthorne's political ambitions remained, however, and at the next election, in 1806, he and John Dent, one of the retiring MPs, were returned unopposed. Apparently Lord Lowther, who had both interest and influence in Lancaster, had been unable to find a candidate to challenge Cawthorne. It seems the latter was regarded as something of a rabble-rouser, much of whose electoral support came from the 'non-respectable' section of the town's freemen who alone had the right to vote. Notwithstanding the fact that he was now back in the House of Commons, Cawthorne discovered that his court-martial conviction and his expulsion had not been forgotten. As a consequence a Commons committee was appointed to look into the circumstances and report back in due course. However, the matter had not been resolved when Parliament was suddenly dissolved in the spring of 1807, thereby precipitating another general election. A bitterly fought nine-day contest then followed in which Cawthorne and his running mate, Gabriel Doveton (a wealthy East Indian Company army officer) were heavily defeated by John Dent and his colleague Peter Patten of Warrington. Cawthorne himself came bottom of the poll – his court-martial conviction being much used against him. Over the next five years Cawthorne retained his prominent position in Lancaster, and in 1807 he started to celebrate his birthday in January of each year with a gift of two bullocks and a quantity of potatoes for a meal for 200, later 400, poor people of the town. He was to continue this habit up until 1823. Whatever Cawthorne's motives, this largesse must have been very welcome to the recipients. At a later stage he donated a plot of land behind his Lancaster house as a site for the new Girls National School. The building, now flats, can still be seen at the corner of Cawthorne Street and High Street with a suitable inscription over the door.

The next general election was in 1812. Both Dent and Patten decided not to stand and, as in 1806, Lord Lowther was unable to find a candidate to represent his interest. As a consequence, Cawthorne and Doveton were elected unopposed. The former indicated that he was ready to support the government but was soon complaining as before that he was getting none of the Lancaster patronage (i.e. appointments in the gift of the government) which were

A NEW SONG

FOR THE ELECTION,

Tune,—*Mistress Casey.*

WHEN CAWTHORNE led a noble Band of Britons stout and steady,
To spill his blood in Freedom's cause each gallant Soul was ready ;
He basely form'd a dark design 'gainst every honest heart, Sirs,
And quitting Virtue's sacred cause, *He* took the Traitor's part, Sirs.
    For this he made his fixed plan,
      That Honour ne'er should bind him ;
    " I'll FILCH,*," said he, where'er I can,*
      Bawl CHURCH AND KING *to blind 'em."*

Their *Marching Guineas* first he seiz'd, for Shoes and Stockings given,
The *shoeless* fellows limp'd away, by pain and anger driven,
To GEN'RAL HOWE they made complaint, who order'd full redress, Sirs,
But *Cawthorne* form'd a deeper scheme to add to their distress, Sirs,
    For this he made &c.

Receipts he got from ev'ry man, as if he then would pay them,
And when they came expecting *Cash,* he boldly did display them,
" See here !" he cried, " the Men's *Receipts,* what knaves are they that ask it,"—
Alas ! the knave is he that cheats, then meanly strives to mask it.
    For this he made &c.

A hundred other tricks he play'd, of fraud and peculation,
Oppressive of THE POOR MAN'S RIGHTS,—injurious to the Nation,
Which ROYAL GEORGE indignant heard, and order'd him to *Trial,*
Where all his *Crimes* of blackest hue, were prov'd beyond denial.
    For this he made &c.

Struck from the *Army, Senate, Bench,* in ev'ry way degraded,
He asks your Votes with *brazen face,* with *Infamy* o'ershaded :
Then shun the Man and spurn his Cause, which ever would disgrace you,
And from the gallant Rolls of Fame ignobly would displace you.
    For this he made &c.

Last time return'd—but freemen why ? He had no opposition :
Once more in vain his Seat he seeks, by this new Coalition ;
And *valour's wreath,* in Britain's cause, a Briton's greatest fame, Sirs,
From DOVETON's brow, he fain would snatch, to hide his own gross shame, Sirs.
    For this he made &c.

The Leopard can he change his spots ? The African his hue, Sirs ?
Or can a DOVETON lend his aid to serve a *Cawthorne's* view, Sirs ?
Can *Honour, Courage,* and *Renown,*—a British Soldier's pride, Sirs,
With *Baseness, Cowardice,* and *Lies,* e'er canvass side by side, Sirs ?
    For this he made &c.

We'll *Vote* for PATTEN and for DENT, in *Freedom's, Honour's* Cause, Sirs,
Untainted keep our *Charter'd Rights,* our *Characters,* our Laws, Sirs ;
So ENGLAND still with plaudits loud, shall record our Renown, Sirs,
And * EDWARD's Shade, without disgrace, still own his fav'rite Town, Sirs.
    For these THEY'VE *made their fixed plans,*
      That HONOUR *still should guide them :*
    Then drink their Cause in FLOWING CANS,
      And ev'ry Good betide them.

---

* Edward III. granted the Charter to the Borough of Lancaster.

CLARK, Printer, Market-Place, Lancaster.

John Fenton Cawthorne's court-martial conviction for dishonesty was regularly used against him in his attempts to be elected as one of Lancaster's MPs. This is from 1807. He lost.

The Girls' Charity School situated on the corner of High Street and Cawthorne Street on land donated by John Fenton Cawthorne in 1813, though the building itself was not erected until seven years later.

PHOTOGRAPH: CARNEGIE

going to Doveton rather than himself. Enquiries indicated that government ministers were 'of the opinion that Cawthorne was such a blackguard they thought it best to have nothing to do with him'. Certainly an unattractive figure of an unscrupulous politician emerges, but perhaps he was little worse than a sizeable proportion of his fellow MPs. At all events, Cawthorne lost his seat again in 1818, recovered it in 1820 and held it until his death in 1831 at the age of 78. It is perhaps significant that Cawthorne was successful in only one contested election and on that occasion his opponent withdrew after having apparently been nominated without his consent.

Of course there was more to Fenton Cawthorne than politics. At Wyreside he had the misfortune to be a near neighbour of David Cragg of Ortner, whom we have already met and who kept a critical eye on Cawthorne's activities.

At the height of the anti-French feeling in early 1793 Cawthorne arranged a ceremonial burning of an effigy of Tom Paine, the well-known radical and something of a political hero to Cragg. The latter commented in his journal, 'Report says there was 1,400 or 1,500 fools there but the greatest fool there was Cawthorne'. In 1796 Cragg received like manna from heaven the news of the court-martial conviction and the subsequent expulsion from the House of Commons: '… So now this tyrant is divested of all his honours and places and reduced to nothing and worse than nothing an infamous character.' The following year Cragg was happy to record that Cawthorne had been threatened with a horsewhipping following a clash over shooting rights with the proprietors of Dolphinholme Mill.

By now Fenton Cawthorne's financial problems had become well known and Cragg was able to report, with some pleasure, 'Cawthorne the tyrant of this neighbourhood has mostly this summer been kept a prisoner in his own house he not daring to stir out for fear of Bailiffs'. As a consequence some land in Skerton and a public house in Lancaster, 'The Grapes', were offered for sale. The death of William Stone, Cawthorne's gamekeeper, gave Cragg another opportunity to vent his spleen. The dead man, who clearly had nothing going for him, was described as 'savage tyrannical and overbearing. Ill-natured curst and wicked. Beloved nor respected by no man.' The diarist seems to have been remarkably well informed because he tells us that Stone had repented on his death bed, admitting that he had been guilty of every sin except murder and 'May his worthy master soon follow because he has done enough'.

Shortly after this incident we find Cragg recording at length and with bleak satisfaction Cawthorne's expensive but unsuccessful attempts to discover coal beneath his Wyreside estate.

Other incidents recorded to Cawthorne's discredit and ultimate discomfiture relate to an abortive attempt to sack the teacher at Abbeystead School and an alleged fraudulent attempt to alter the boundaries of some land that was being sold. Finally there was the account of the lengthy dispute which began when Cawthorne (and one of his employees) confiscated a gun which was being carried, by one Peter Tomlinson who had had the gun for repair, along a public footpath which crossed Cawthorne's land. This matter dragged on and ultimately Cawthorne (and his employee) were convicted of assault at Lancaster Assizes and each fined 6s. 8d, a common sum at the time for a petty misdemeanour or affray. It is perhaps indicative of Cawthorne's popularity and reputation among his fellow gentry that is is quite clear that Tomlinson was encouraged to take legal action (and possibly given financial support) by none other than Lord Archibald Hamilton of Ashton Hall, close relative of the

Duke of Hamilton and the biggest landowner in north Lancashire. It is to be regretted that Cragg's diary (or at least that part available to us) dries up soon after this last incident. Nevertheless, he survived Fenton Cawthorne, who died childless in 1831 – still MP for Lancaster. An account of his country house, Wyreside Hall, appears in the *Lonsdale Magazine* for 1821. It is a somewhat fawning article, but it does make clear that like so many of his contemporaries he was very interested in agricultural improvements and that he obviously spent time and money on the bettering of his estates. Nevertheless he cannot be described as a likeable person. His funeral at Lancaster parish church appears to have been well attended and the pall-bearers were all members of the local gentry. Death is a great time for forgiveness![1]

Wyreside Hall near Dolphinholme, about ten miles from Lancaster, was the residence of John Fenton Cawthorne who was for many years a local MP.

FROM LONSDALE MAGAZINE 2. REPRODUCED BY PERMISSION OF THE COUNTY ARCHIVIST, LANCASHIRE RECORD OFFICE

William White

William White was born in 1758 at Lancaster, the son of Henry White and Mary Cawthorne. As a consequence he was related to John Fenton Cawthorne. He went to school at Sedbergh before going on to Clare College, Cambridge, in 1777. He seems to have left Cambridge without taking a degree but was re-admitted in 1790, graduating three years later and taking up his MA in 1796.

However, he had already been appointed vicar of Lancaster in 1794 in succession to his brother-in-law, Oliver Marton of Capernwray, near Carnforth, whose family owned the advowson or the right to appoint to the living of the parish church of Lancaster. In this instance the actual appointment was made by the executors of the appropriate member of the Marton family – one of whom just happened to be John Fenton Cawthorne! Many aspects of public life were extremely incestuous in those days. It was indeed common practice in the eighteenth and early nineteenth centuries for owners of a church living to bestow this upon a member of the family or a close friend – the idea of seeking out the best candidate did not often arise – the advowson was a piece of property which could be bought and sold and the way it was used (or misused) was at the entire whim of the owner and nothing whatever to do with anybody else. It has to be admitted that William White was not the best of vicars, although our friend David Cragg records a charitable gift of two guineas made by 'Parson White' in 1800. From 1801 when the *Lancaster Gazette* was first published there is no mention of him in the paper. His duties (even civic ceremonies) appear to have been performed by a succession of curates. Indeed, in a letter written in 1805 White himself says, 'It is five and a half years since I was at Lancaster'. How or where he spent his time when away from Lancaster is not clear, although he had a sister and a niece both living in the vicinity with whom he kept in touch and a Mr John Park, a local solicitor, looked after his affairs, including property owned by him. His sister, Mrs Saul, and niece, Mrs Harrison, were active socially in Lancaster. The *Lancaster Gazette* reported in January 1802 that they gave 'an elegant ball and supper to a numerous assemblage of beauty and fashion. The ball was opened by Mrs Hunter and Lord Strathmore.' The latter had taken a short lease of Wyreside Hall from John Fenton Cawthorne.

As has already been mentioned, in 1802/03 there was a lull in the war with France. As a consequence travel to the continent became, once again, a possibility and many people took the opportunity to visit France and particularly to go to Paris to see for themselves the situation there after the turmoil and bloodshed of the revolutionary years. William White, still a bachelor, was one of these visitors and his natural curiosity led to his ultimate downfall. Despite a worsening diplomatic position in the early months of 1803 many hundreds of visitors ignored the warning signs and, as a consequence, were still in France when war was declared in May of that year. Ordinarily, this would not have been a problem as private citizens would have been permitted to return home in their own time notwithstanding the outbreak of hostilities. However, Napoleon Bonaparte, First Consul of France and soon to be Emperor, was enraged by what he regarded as premature attacks by the Royal Navy on French shipping and ordered the immediate detention and internment of all (male) British citizens still in France. Unfortunately Reverend William White was one of these persons and he soon found himself being dispatched with many others to the fortress town of Verdun in eastern France. This unprecedented action by the French government caused anger and consternation in Great Britain and much diplomatic pressure was exerted to have the internees released. In most cases these representations were to no avail, although strings were pulled successfully for a few lucky internees; the unfortunate vicar of Lancaster was not among this select few. The majority of those interned had therefore to remain in a loose form of detention until the end of the war in 1814, one example being a Mr John Maude of Kendal who did not return home until May of that year.

There have survived four letters from Verdun written by William White to his niece and sister at Kendal and Lancaster, dated between May 1804 and February 1806. Like all prisoners and expatriates he was desperate for information from home and he reproaches his correspondents for not writing frequently enough and not describing all the gossip from Lancaster. Some letters from England seem to have gone astray and he complains to his niece that he had not heard from his solicitor, Mr Park, for almost a year or from a Mr Thomas on church business either. Of these church duties he says little, though in his first letter he writes, 'Have the goodness to give directions that when the Bishop comes to Lancaster apartments may be fitted up for him at the Vicarage.' The Vicarage (then situated opposite the east end of the church) appears to have been let by White as he refers to his

> fair tenant and quondam flirt ... and when I was informed that my health had been drunk in one of her nocturnal revels I did not fail to return it by wishing her, silently, in a bumper, all the happiness that this transitory life is capable of.

Memorial in the Priory Church, Lancaster, to Reverend William White, the
unfortunate vicar of Lancaster who died a prisoner in France, in 1806, a victim of the
French Wars.

PHOTOGRAPH: CARNEGIE

Later in the same letter White asks his sister to enquire of Mr Park '… if the cellar at the Vicarage is and always has been properly secured and if he knows what quantity of wine, etc., there is in it'. William White, unlike some of his fellow detainees, clearly had sufficient funds to make his enforced stay in France reasonably comfortable but despite the rather pompous and patronising comments in some of his letters it is easy to feel sorry for him when he writes in July 1805

> For a person who does not drink champaign [*sic*] and has no passion for horseracing … this is a most wretched place. I don't speak of our treatment, which, considering our situation, is good. But being deprived of the power of moving at will is an evil that to be known must be experienced. With respect to myself, I live in very good lodgings in the house of the Mayor of the Town and for the summer months have taken a couple of rooms (which look into a garden) at a village about a league off …

The last surviving letter is not by William White but from a friend also detained at Verdun named Alexander Allen, who seems to have been a doctor. He describes the illness and final demise of White, who died during the summer of 1806. 'His funeral was most respectable, the service was read by the Rev'd Mr Gordon. He is interred in the Cimetière de St Medard situated at the North East part of the town. I have caused a gravestone to be placed over him with the following description "W. White M.A. Vicar of Lancaster. Died 14th June 1806 Aged 48 years".'

William White was succeeded as vicar of Lancaster by the Reverend John Manby, a former chaplain to the Duke of Sussex, one of the sons of George III. The appointment was made by the Crown as the then head of the Marton family had become insane and was adjudged incapable of exercising his rights as the owner of the living. It appears to have been a good choice and the new vicar was most diligent and conscientious in the performance of his duties although somewhat litigous and, most importantly, resided in his parish and became heavily involved in local life. A memorial to his unfortunate predecessor was affixed at the request of his niece to the interior of the south wall of the parish church, where it can still be seen today.[2]

Charles Gibson

Charles Gibson was the fourth son of the Reverend John Gibson and was born in 1760. The Gibson estate was at Myerscough, between Garstang and Preston,

Charles Gibson 1760–1823 of
Quernmore Park near Lancaster.

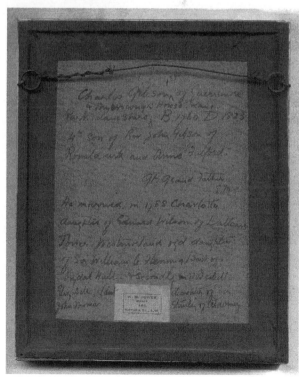

Quernmore Park, between Caton and Lancaster, the residence of Charles Gibson, the
leading local citizen for the period of this book.

FROM LONSDALE MAGAZINE 3. REPRODUCED BY PERMISSION OF THE COUNTY ARCHIVIST,
LANCASHIRE RECORD OFFICE

but over the years considerable additional property was added either through
purchase or inheritance – in Lancaster, Preston, Westmorland, Durham and
the Furness area of Lancashire.

Charles Gibson himself was educated at a school near Chester but as far
as is known he did not proceed to any form of further education; certainly
he did not attend either Oxford or Cambridge.

Two years after the death of his father in 1786 he was married well and
appropriately to Charlotte Wilson, the daughter of Edward Wilson of Dallam
Tower, Milnthorpe in Westmorland, and an elder son, also called Charles,
was born in 1790. It seems that at this time the family lived in Church Street,
Lancaster, in a now demolished house the site of which is currently occupied
by the National Westminster Bank.

At some time in the 1780s, probably 1786, Charles Gibson agreed to buy the 1,300-acre Quernmore Park estate, between Lancaster and Caton, from Lord Clifford whose family had owned the property for the previous 120 years. There were long delays (partly due to the death of Lord Clifford) before the purchase was finally completed in 1794 at a cost of £21,000. Almost immediately a new residence was commissioned (the architect was probably Thomas Harrison who designed the new Skerton Bridge over the Lune, completed in 1788). The building was sufficiently far advanced for the family to move in in 1795, completion following three years later. The landscaping and laying out of the garden then followed under the direction of a Mr Webb.

Aspects of Charles Gibson's public life have already been mentioned. He was Lieutenant of the Lonsdale Division of the County, Commander of the Original Lancaster Volunteers Regiment and also a magistrate and high sheriff of Lancashire in 1798. Otherwise it seems likely that one of his main interests was in agriculture. From the initiative provided by Thomas Coke of Holkham in Norfolk and more locally by John Christian Curwen in West Cumberland and Westmorland the late eighteenth and early nineteenth centuries were the great period of the agricultural improver. It became fashionable for the more sober and intelligent of the landed gentry to improve their estates with new techniques of ploughing, draining, manuring, choice of crops and improved livestock breeding. Tenants were encouraged by the terms of their leases to adopt the latest fashions in agriculture and both they and their landlords met on amicable if not equal terms at the new agricultural societies which were formed all over the country. The Lancaster Agricultural Society came into existence in 1797 and the first president was Charles Gibson himself, a position he kept on and off for the next twenty years or so. It was a connection that Gibson faithfully maintained for the rest of his life, frequently being named as a prizewinner in one or more of the various classifications at the annual show held in Dalton Square. After the prize giving at the Town Hall had been completed the members would adjourn to Miss Noon's, the proprietor of the Royal Oak Hotel in Market Square, a noted hostelry (where the Public Library now stands), for dinner where 'the evening was chiefly spent in discussions on agricultural subjects interspersed with toasts and songs'.

Agricultural improvements at Quernmore in particular related to the construction of new farm buildings both for tenants and the home farm, the breeding of shorthorn cattle and the planting of many thousands of trees. Gibson was one of the prime movers behind the 1811 Act for the enclosure of Quernmore Waste from which he benefited to the extent of over six hundred acres. This allocation of land involved heavy fencing, walling and road-making obligations together with the substantial cost of improving the land. There is anecdotal evidence from the family, which records Gibson saying to his son, 'It will pay, my son, though it may never pay me.' The financial drain on the estate of all the accumulated improvements as well as the necessity to provide for members of the family was an undoubted burden which remained until the estate was subsequently sold.

Gibson was clearly a man of both culture and ability, with an inventive turn of mind. He developed a cattle-weighing machine and a water-powered threshing machine which, intriguingly, was later used to blow the bellows of an organ installed in the breakfast room at Quernmore Park. Gibson was proficient on the organ as well as the flute and violincello and enjoyed wood turning and inlaying. In religion he was an Anglican and in politics a supporter of William Pitt (party labels such as Whig or Tory meant less than they do now), one of the comparatively few statesmen of principle and ability that the period produced. Gibson was a founder member of the local Pitt Club formed to commemorate and support Pitt's political beliefs. He was also a firm supporter of John Dent, MP for Lancaster between 1790 and 1812, whose candidature he could always be found supporting at election times. Not surprisingly, then, on no occasion is there any record of Gibson giving any support to John Fenton Cawthorne.

On a wider level Charles Gibson seems to have been well liked. Jonathan Binns, a Quaker who farmed at Leech House between Lancaster and Galgate, refers twice in his autobiography to 'my friend Charles Gibson'. Binns was secretary to the Lancaster Agricultural Society for some years and though from a very respectable background (his father was a doctor) he was clearly not 'gentry'. Nevertheless, he had a good relationship with Gibson, who tried to help Binns find a new farm tenancy and also arranged for him to be given an introduction to the famous agriculturalist Coke of Holkham. He was a regular subscriber to charity and founded a kind of evening school for children at Quernmore Park as well as a Sunday School in which his wife helped.

Charles Gibson's first wife died in 1807. He was re-married five years later to Isabella Stanley, the daughter of Sir John Stanley of Alderley in Cheshire. In accordance with his public and social position he seems to have been involved in local society and during the twice yearly assizes he entertained from time to time the judges and barristers attending the court. He also sat regularly on the grand jury, which then performed certain legal obligations at the start of each assize.

Charles Gibson died in 1823, having the previous year sustained serious losses in the collapse of the Worswick Bank at Lancaster – apparently in

SACRED
TO THE MEMORY OF
CHARLES GIBSON,
LATE OF *QUERMORE PARK*, ESQUIRE,
WHO DEPARTED THIS LIFE ON THE 16ᵗʰ DAY OF JUNE 1823,
IN THE 63ᵗ YEAR OF HIS AGE,
AND LIES INTERRED IN THE PARISH CHURCH AT LANCASTER,
WHERE A MONUMENT TO HIS MEMORY HAS BEEN ERECTED BY HIS ELDEST SON,
CHARLES GIBSON, NOW OF *QUERMORE PARK*, ESQUIRE.
HE MARRIED (24ᵗʰ JANᵞ 1788) CHARLOTTE, YOUNGEST DAUGHTER OF
EDWARD WILSON, OF *DALLAM TOWER*, IN THE COUNTY OF WESTMORLAND, ESQUIRE,
(BY WHOM HE LEFT ISSUE FOUR SONS,
VIZ, THE ABOVE NAMED CHARLES, AND JOHN, EDWARD AND ROBERT,
AND TWO DAUGHTERS, CHARLOTTE AND DOROTHY,)
AND, SECONDLY, (19ᵗʰ DECᵞ 1812) ISABELLA ELIZABETH, ELDEST DAUGHTER OF
SIR JOHN THOMAS STANLEY OF *ALDERLEY*,
IN THE COUNTY OF CHESTER, BARONET,
WHO SURVIVING HIM, HAS CAUSED THIS TABLET TO BE ERECTED,
AS A MONUMENT OF HER IRREPARABLE LOSS,
AND A TRIBUTE OF AFFECTION AND REGARD TO HER
DEPARTED HUSBAND, AND HIS FAMILY.

The Gibson (of Quernmore Park) memorial in Brookhouse church near Lancaster. Early deaths and the economic burden of a large family probably contributed to the sale of the estate in the early 1840s.

PHOTOGRAPH: CARNEGIE

excess of £4,000, a huge sum in those days. He was succeeded by his eldest son, also called Charles, who died young in 1832, leaving nine children. Both father and son are buried in the priory church at Lancaster, though there is also a memorial in Brookhouse Church. Much of the family subsequently emigrated to New Zealand, where their descendants still live. The Quernmore Park estate was purchased by the Garnett family in 1842, to whom, with the exception of the mansion, some of it still belongs.

The picture of Charles Gibson which emerges from contemporary records is quite an attractive one, and he seems to have been a gentleman in every sense of the word as well as being liked and respected by all; for his time he was the best type of progressive landowner. We can perhaps conclude this study of him by quoting at length from the *Lancaster Gazette* for 17 October 1801, which dealt in part with the local celebrations to mark the treaty which led to the eighteen-month cessation of hostilities known as the Peace of Amiens.

At Quarmore [sic] Park, near this town, the seat of Charles Gibson Esq., the Colonel of the Loyal Lancaster Volunteers, the Peace was celebrated with much festivity on Tuesday evening. The tenants, workmen and labourers assembled round a large bonfire, where two barrels of excellent ale were brought for them to drink a number of suitable toasts. A small transparency was exhibited with the words 'King George the Third' and 'Peace'. A [representation] of a Cottage Fireside and the Aqueduct had a pleasing effect. 'God Save the King' was repeatedly sung and the enthusiasm with which the health of the worthy donor and his family was drunk shewed how the hearts of all glowed with affection and esteem.

Cloying slightly, overdrawn undoubtedly, nevertheless it is a pleasing and probably not inaccurate picture of events in that rather less sophisticated age.[3]

CHAPTER TEN

Hardship and tragedy

O NE recurring feature of life in Lancaster throughout the whole period of the war was the passage of troops through the town. Sometimes they stayed for a period of time but other times either only overnight or they merely marched through the town *en route* to some other destination. The fact that Lancaster was situated on the main north–south road was of course the main reason for this military presence. Kendal was in the same position and an anonymous diarist living there in the early nineteenth century recorded with pleasure the frequent passage of regular and militia units – preferably with a band of music.[1] Proceedings at the quarter sessions held in Lancaster record many payments to local contractors for transporting regimental baggage from Lancaster to Preston or from Lancaster to Kendal – there were twelve such payments in 1794 alone, and eight the following year.[2]

North-west England was of course not alone in this. Linda Colley in her book *Britons*[3] cites the example of Woodbridge in Suffolk which, at different times over the years, played host to twenty-seven different regiments. She makes the point that civilians in these garrison towns 'found themselves suddenly and regularly brought into contact with Britons possessed of different kinds of accents and vocabularies, different cultural backgrounds and leisure practices and from very different places'. One can only guess what effect all this had on the local inhabitants as well as the soldiers. At the very least it would inform all those involved that there was a wider world out there consisting of both peoples and places of which both sides hitherto knew little or nothing.

In 1807 and 1808 there were visits to Lancaster from the Royal Cornwall Militia. These proved very popular. The *Lancaster Gazette* reported:

The three divisions of the Royal Cornwall Militia arrived in this town
on Monday, Tuesday and Wednesday last … An excellent band of music
accompanied the first division and the amateurs were entertained with several
select pieces on Monday evening in Dalton Square.

Lancashire, To the Constable of the Township of *Skerton*
to wit. in the said County.

IN Pursuance of an Order from *the Secretary of War*
this Day brought and shewn unto me *John Bradshaw*
Esquire one of his Majesty's
Justices of the Peace, in and for the said County, by *Gavin*
Hutchison Serjeant in the 71st Regiment of
Foot commanded by *Lieutenant Halpass*
I do hereby require you to provide within your
Constablewick *One* sufficient Carriages with Horses,
and able Men to drive the same, whereby to remove the Arms, Clothes and
Accoutrements of the said *Regiment* now on their
March from *Carlisle* to *Hilton*
in the *Hampshire*
and with them you are to appear at *the King's arms*
in Lancaster aforesaid, on *Saturday* precisely at *three*
o'Clock in *the Morning* Herein fail not under the
Penalty thereon to issue. Given under my Hand and Seal, at Lancaster
aforesaid, this *second* Day of *July* one
thousand *eight hundred and thirteen*

John Bradshaw

Garston

Orders to provide transport for military baggage continued throughout the whole of the war. This from July 1813 relates to a detachment of the 7th Foot (now part of the Royal Regiment of Fusiliers) *en route* from Carlisle to Hampshire and then probably to Spain.

QSP 2644/57 AND QSP 2644/58. REPRODUCED BY PERMISSION OF THE COUNTY ARCHIVIST, LANCASHIRE RECORD OFFICE

Skerton July 13 1813

Mr Richd Johnson County Treasurer
To the Constable of Skerton Dr

To Removing the Arms Cloaths & Accoutrements
of the 7th Regiment of Foot from Lancaster
to Garstang one Horse — £0 . 1 . 4½

Richd Hall Constable
13th July 1813.
Allowed by —
Rob. Houman

The Cornwall Militia came to Lancaster again in July of the following year, this time heading south. They stayed some weeks and made themselves most agreeable to Lancastrians by organising a two-day wrestling contest among their own men, with a purse of guineas going to the winner. The *Gazette* assured its readers that 'this manly display of skill, strength and activity was witnessed by a crowd of spectators'. A few days later it was reported that:

> The Royal Cornwall Militia pitched their tents on Lancaster Moor on Wednesday last and went through a number of manoeuvres and evolutions with the greatest precision and correctness. Great numbers of people went to view the encampment during the day and were much surprised at the quick manner in which the men struck the tents in the evening and returned to the town.

This activity was repeated a few weeks later, with another full account in the *Gazette* for 30 July:

> On Thursday morning, the Royal Cornwall Militia, commanded by Colonel Williams now lying here, marched to the Moor and again pitched their tents for the day. So novel a sight as an encampment attracted a great number of spectators from this town and neighbourhood.

The reporter then lost all control of himself and went on:

> In the evening a number of ladies and gentlemen having partaken of refreshments in the Colonel's marquee led the merry dance on the green sod, nor did they depart till 'the sable goddess' threw her mantle around them.

The Cornwall Militia followed this up with a band concert at the Assembly Rooms in King Street in early August before finally leaving the town at the end of that month. Lancaster must have missed them.

Between March and May 1813 no fewer than four Scottish militia regiments passed through Lancaster, sometimes staying overnight, and three militia regiments from Ireland did likewise. Other units involved in that year were the 7th Dragoons and two regiments of Hampshire militia. The South Hampshires stayed in and about Lancaster for several months (the officers were in a house on Castle Hill belonging to Doctor Campbell) and on their departure they were congratulated by the local paper for their good behaviour.

Soldiers on the march were usually billeted in local inns and public houses, and there was a legal liability upon innkeepers to provide food and accommodation. This was a very unpopular and unprofitable duty and one expects that the men would be told to sleep in the stables and given very basic food from the sum allowed to the innkeeper from public funds. They most certainly would not be allowed to mix with the ordinary paying guests. The problems which could arise were illustrated in January 1808 at Burton-in-Kendal when the Ayrshire Militia attempted to find lodging in the four inns of that village. Accommodation was found somehow, but one inn had over 100 soldiers under its roof. Some ten years earlier in the spring of 1798 our friend David Cragg had noted:

> There are about eight hundred [supplementary] Militia at Lancaster and some soldiers beside. All the town is full of them. At the King's Arms sixty-one billeted, at the New Inn [in Market Street] forty-five, the Bear and Staff [in Penny Street] thirty-five, the Boar's Head twenty and White Cross Toll Bars sixteen, etc., etc. It is supposed they will march from Lancaster before the Assizes begin.

Despite the low level of the official billeting allowances payable to innkeepers (though it was increased to 2*d.* per man per day in 1813), the regular military visits to Lancaster cannot have been entirely unpopular. Apart from the free entertainment, several hundred soldiers and their better-off officers must have spent a considerable amount of money in the town – mainly on food and drink but other things as well, all of which would in some way have helped to sustain the local economy during some of the hard wartime years.

However, not all the visits of the military to Lancaster were as friendly as those described above. Some were very much in the line of duty and were associated with hardship and tragedy. In 1795, 1796 and finally in January 1800 there was a series of food riots in Lancaster. All these were caused by the high prices of basic foodstuffs following bad harvests. Similar and usually more serious disturbances took place all across the country. Certainly during the earlier riots of 1795 and 1796 the rioters were more concerned with seizing quantities of food – in the North West usually oatmeal and potatoes rather than wheat, and then selling them on to the crowd at what seemed fairer prices. This was an example of the so-called 'moral economy' (of much interest to historians) and a reaction not only against high prices but also against the perceived profiteering activities of corn merchants, factors and middlemen. Almost inevitably David Cragg was present on the 8th August 1795 at the regular market held on the ground floor of the Town Hall in Market Square and he says that disturbances were started by a number of 'raggetty women'.

Apparently a man named Taylor from Borwick was offering oatmeal at 52s. 6d. and then 50s. per load of 240 pounds. There were no takers and Taylor was in the process of taking it away when 'a mad woman' pulled a sack off his back. About forty other women joined in (including one Rebecca Ashton of Wyresdale), the meal was taken out into the street and sold off in small amounts equivalent to 40s. per load. Robert Addison, the mayor, was called to the scene together with two colleagues but they were 'jostled and joweled' and could do nothing and were unable to restore order.

There was another disturbance the following January outside the Bear and Staff in Penny Street adjacent to Horse Shoe Corner, where a cart full of oatmeal had been left. Cragg reported, however, that it was left untouched after the angry crowd was told by a countryman, 'if they wanted to go to the Castle they might lay hands on it – if not they had better desist for if anyone made any attempt to unload it they would certainly go there or to the House of Correction [at Preston].' The following day a crowd broke into Redmayne's warehouse, found some meal but took nothing. They then moved down Pudding Lane (Cheapside) on to the Quay, where they broke some windows. According to Cragg, what infuriated the crowd was the sight of many carts of oatmeal from South Westmorland passing straight through Lancaster to other destinations, particularly in south and east Lancashire.

The most serious incident took place four years later on 25 January 1800. Cragg describes the background:

> There never was perhaps so much cause to fear a famine or at least a great dearth of corn as at the present period, from the backwardness of last spring and the unparalleled coldness and wetness of last summer which caused a universal failure in the crop of corn of all sorts. The farmers have thrashed upon the whole more than usual of their crops at this time and sold all the meal that has been made.

Our diarist does not seem to have been personally present on the 25th, but was able to give a full account in his journal, presumably gathered from an actual eyewitness. He was even able to correct his original account a few days later, so it seems likely that his account is, broadly speaking, accurate. As before, the disturbance started in the grain market at the town hall when one of the oatmeal dealers was asking more than the market price and as a consequence could make no sale. The dealer then reportedly expressed the hope that the price would rise to £5 per load by the end of the month; alternatively, and surely more likely, he said that he would not be at all surprised if it reached that price. Either way, his remarks not unnaturally infuriated the crowd of would-be purchasers; a sack of oatmeal was then seized, torn open and divided out among the crowd at the rate of 6 pounds of meal for a shilling. It so happened that there was a party of dragoons in town (probably the 17th Light Dragoons who were stationed in north Lancashire for about three years at the turn of the century) and it seems that these then entered the town hall and drove out the crowd. After about three hours it was decided to remove the remaining meal to the Bear and Staff Inn in a cart driven by a man named Ralph Parker, who was given a military escort for the journey. Cragg then takes up the story:

> At Penny Street, about the Bear and Staff a vast crowd of people collected together and the Dragoons rode through them many times which caused great thrutching and bustling among them and many were forced against the sides by the press of the crowd and the windows on both sides of the street were broken by people being forced against them. There is mention of one or two being hurt or ridden [on] by the Dragoon horses. The owner of the meal was guarded out of town by the soldiers and the mob followed after and pelted him with mud and stones.

Interestingly, writing seven years later, Christopher Clark in his *History of Lancaster* confirmed that in the early part of the year 1800 the price of oatmeal did indeed rise to £5 a load. Despite such high, near-famine prices, it was not until early May that a committee for the relief of the poor was set up. The names of many of the members of the committee are already familiar: Richard Gillow, the furniture maker, John Brockbank, the shipbuilder; others were James Booth, the chief customs officer, the Reverend Houseman from St Ann's church in Moor Lane and Thomas Shepherd and Thomas Giles, both future mayors of the town. From the funds supplied it was decided to buy potatoes and re-sell them on at ½d. per pound. Meat, rice and oatmeal were also to be purchased in sufficient quantity to make 800 quarts of soup to be sold at ½d. per quart to those in need evidenced by possession of a ticket, presumably issued by the poor law overseers. This soup kitchen/discount shop operated from the town hall, with the potatoes being stored in the cellar, and remained in being until early August 1800 before being wound up and final accounts prepared. It must have been of inestimable benefit to many of the town's poorest families.[4]

The disturbances of 1812 were a very different matter; although Lancaster was only affected indirectly, this was in a sensational and tragic manner. The events of 1812 were on a very large scale and for a time considerable sections of Lancashire and Yorkshire were in a state of virtual insurrection. Often described as the Luddite rising after the name of its mythical leader 'General' Ned Ludd, the anger of the rioters was levelled at the gradual mechanisation of industrial processes. Matters were made worse by a severe rise in food prices and a general economic deterioration arising from the stagnation of trade and the loss of overseas markets in Europe due to the never-ending war and the rupture of trade relations with the United States. The violent attacks on machinery began among the hosiery workers of the East Midlands and then spread to the woollen districts of the West Riding and finally to the industrial areas of south Lancashire and north Cheshire. All in all these disturbances were probably the most severe this country has faced in the last 250 years. With a world war to fight, the British government clearly had no option but to quell the unrest with a firm if not ruthless series of measures and as a consequence many thousands of additional troops (mainly regular cavalry and militia infantry) were moved into the disturbed areas. As an exercise in repression the measures taken by the government were, broadly speaking, successful although the cost was high in individual suffering and loss of life – the latter resulting from the inevitable collisions between the rioters and the military as well as the judicial processes which took place at the assizes at Chester, York and Lancaster. Where the government failed was in its over-reaction to events and its lack of understanding and humanity in taking no steps to mitigate the very genuine underlying hardships.

In late April the first prisoners – twenty-five men and four women under an escort of the Scots Greys – arrived at Lancaster Castle from the Manchester area. Use of regular soldiers for this purpose was unusual, justified only by the seriousness of the situation. A few days later two companies of the Berkshire Militia arrived from Preston, where they were currently stationed. As was usual, in May the Lonsdale Local Militia was called out for its annual training and on this occasion was to some extent used in a security role, with the *Gazette* reporting: 'On the 15th and 16th instant several ships' guns were removed from different warehouses in this town by the Local Militia to their guardhouse at the Castle.' In addition, they mounted a permanent guard of 'two centries' at the main gate of the castle for three weeks until relieved by sixty men of the Royal Horse Guards on 30 May. The local militia, 'a fine body of men', were then stood down.

There was no actual rioting in Lancaster itself, but in the middle of May a break-in occurred at premises near the Green Area (later the site of the now demolished Green Ayre Station). The thieves took 50s. in money and a bottle of rum and left behind a note signed 'General Ludd'. Perhaps this news gave a few of the more nervous citizens of Lancaster a sleepless night. More serious and perhaps more indicative of the national feelings of unrest was an attempt to block the main turnpike road leading northwards from Lancaster. An appropriate notice appeared in the *Lancaster Gazette*:

> Whereas some evil disposed persons on the night of the 30th April last placed eleven gates across the Turnpike Road between the second and third milestone from Lancaster towards Burton-in-Kendal whereby the lives of his Majesty's subjects and the destruction of the Mail Coach and Horses was endangered.

A substantial £50 reward was offered for the apprehension of the guilty persons. Interference with the Royal Mail was always regarded as a very serious matter.

Lancaster Assizes were held in March and August of each year but an additional court, known as a Special Commission of Assize, to try the Manchester rioters was opened on 23 May. The trials were completed by the end of the month and eight people – seven men and one woman – were sentenced to death for offences of arson and stealing bread, cheese and potatoes, together with seventeen others who were each sentenced to seven years' transportation to Australia. All the offences had been committed in south Lancashire. Usually many of those sentenced to death were reprieved, but on this occasion it is clear that the judges and the other authorities were determined that an example should be made – as indeed it was. On 13 June 1812, 'before a vast concourse of people', the executions took place behind the Castle and

> a troop of Blues [Royal Horse Guards] attended the place of execution and four companies of Berkshire Militia were under arms during the awful scene but we are happy to state that not the least symptoms of tumult appeared … in the morning after the execution their bodies were decently interred.

The proper behaviour of the condemned both in the prison and on the scaffold was always a matter of concern in early nineteenth-century England. Accordingly the *Lancaster Gazette* was able to report:

> We have the authority of the Reverend Mr Rowley, chaplain of the Castle, for assuring our readers that during the whole time after receiving sentence they behaved with the utmost decorum appearing truly penitent and

repeatedly wishing that their untimely fate would prove a warning to those who had broken the laws and cause them to refrain from their evil ways.

Although there were many other multiple executions both before and after this date at Lancaster, the impression emerges that the events of 13 June 1812 were unique in the eyes of the townspeople. Even Jonathan Binns, who in his autobiography ignores most public happenings, refers to these executions. With hindsight it can be seen that the hangings and transportations at Chester, Lancaster and finally York broke the spirit of the insurrection and the improving economic situation in the latter part of the year removed most of the danger. However, throughout the rest of 1812 the price of foodstuffs remained very high, with oatmeal varying between 70s. a load in May to 99s. in August. It did not return to its former level of 40s. until the following year. Again a public meeting was called to plan emergency measures and over £600 were raised by a house-to-house collection to assist the many people then in distress.

Although not fully appreciated at the time, the military situation in Spain had finally changed for the better and the initiative had passed to the British, Spanish and Portuguese forces, starting with the fall of Ciudad Rodrigo in January 1812, continuing with the desperate and bloody storm of Badajoz in April and culminating in the great victory at Salamanca in the high summer of that year; this victory was celebrated in Lancaster, with church bells being rung and flags displayed. Of even more importance was the Napoleonic invasion of Russia in June 1812 which, by the end of the year, had resulted in the almost complete destruction of the French army and the Russian advance into eastern Europe. While 1812 had been a tragic year for northern England, the following year showed signs that the worst might be over.

The Assembly Rooms, King Steet. Erected 1759.
The venue for balls, recitals, concerts and other social events.

CHAPTER ELEVEN

The bitterness of victory and the end of old Lancaster

B Y 1813 the country had been at war with France for virtually twenty years. However, at long last the military and political situation had changed. Fatally wounded by the defeat in Russia, for the French the war in the east went from bad to worse. The Russian army, now joined by a rejuvenated Prussia and Austria, advanced slowly but inexorably across Germany towards the Rhine and France itself. In October the French suffered a catastrophic defeat at the Battle of Leipzig, and in Spain Wellington's army with their Spanish and Portuguese allies had triumphed at Vittoria in June. A few weeks later they stood on the crest of the Pyrenees looking down into France. At home a record harvest, falling food prices and the re-opening of trade with eastern Europe transformed the economic situation. The *Lancaster Gazette* reported that the shortage of labour in the south of the county was such that rewards were being offered for the recruitment of spinners, weavers and dyers. True, shipping losses to French and American privateers still continued and Lancaster ships were not immune. The *Brothers* was launched from Smiths' yard in Skerton in June 1813 but was taken later that year by an American ship off Norway while on her maiden voyage to the Baltic. Better news came on 14 August, with the local paper announcing: 'On Thursday last the ships *Abram*, *Sterling* and *Lancaster* arrived at this port and yesterday got safe into Glasson Dock. They sailed with a fleet of about two hundred sail on the 3rd July from St Thomas.'

All the good news from Spain and the continent doubtless helped the social scene and at the beginning of September the *Gazette* reported:

> Our Theatre opened on Saturday night and has been remarkably well attended, particularly on Tuesday evening ... when the house exhibited such a galaxy of beauty and fashion as can have seldom been equalled.

EIGHTY POUNDS REWARD.
HIGHWAY ROBBERY.
WHEREAS ROBERT SKIRROW, of
Arkholme, in the county of Lancaster,
cattle dealer, on WEDNESDAY night, the 27th
October last, between seven and eight o'clock, was
stopped, by two men, at the Bridge Stone, near
High-Long Ridge, in the highway, on Gressingham
Moor (three miles from Arkholme) and ROBBED
of various NOTES, SILVER, and COPPER, to
the amount of 69l. 11s. 11d. and also of THREE
POCKET MEMORANDUM BOOKS
One of the men is a tall stout man, and had on
a light-coloured coat; the other is a less, broad-set
man, and had on a dark-coloured coat.
*** Whoever apprehends the above robbers, or
either of them, will, on conviction, be entitled to
a REWARD of FORTY POUNDS, for each
robber.
LANCASTER, OCT. 28, 1813.

Serious crime in north Lancashire (as distinct from the south of the county) seems to have been fairly rare. The sum involved here – almost £700 – was enormous by contemporary standards and is indicative of the very prosperous state of agriculture towards the end of the war. The sum lost (or stolen) at Garstang Cattle Fair the following year was even larger. The perpetrators were arrested in a brothel in Bristol, brought back to Lancaster, and sentenced to transportation for life at the March 1815 Assizes.

LOST, OUT OF THE POCKET OF A PERSON,
AT GARSTANG FAIR;
On TUESDAY the 22d day of NOVEMBER, 1814,
The following BANK of ENGLAND and other NOTES:

BANK POST BILLS.

Date	Number.	Signed.	Entered.	To whom payable.	Amt.
4th Nov. 1814,	M. 5704,	C. Phillips,	P. C. J. Brent,	Messrs. Cunliffes and Co.	£100
4th,	M. 6219,	I. Clark,	J. Twiss,	Ditto,	100
9th Oct.	L. 2259,	I. Footh,	C. Hamilton,	Messrs. Pedders and Co.	50
6th Nov.	M. 5699,	C. Phillips,	P. C. J. Brent,	Messrs. Cunliffes and Co.	50
7 October, 1813,	J. I. Booth,		J. Twiss,	James Lee, Esq.	50
7th Aug.	T. 158,	T. Donovan,	P. C. J. Brent,	Messrs. Hobhouse and Co.	50
7 Oct. 1814,	L. 47,	I. Booth,	Ditto,	Messrs. Pedders and Co.	80
9th May, 1813,	P. 4581,	I. Footh,	T. Heultise,	J. Smith, Esq. and Co.	20
9st Oct 1814,	M. 2129,	I. Hogben,	J. Twiss,	Messrs. Cunliffes and Co.	20
					50
					£460

BANK NOTES.

9th Oct. 1814,	4708,	I. Fleetwood,	— — —		25
7 August,	15642,	W. Harris,	— — —		25
9th May,	17014,	Ditto,	— — —		30
9 Nov.	12059,	I. Booth,	— — —		30
9th July,	15922,	T. S. R. West,	— — —		20
9th Sept.	18038,	C. Oliver,	— — —		30
9st June,	6803,	Ditto,	— — —		20
7th Aug.	3074,	Ditto,	— — —		30
9th Jan.	18439,	T. Kensal,	— — —		30
9th Aug.	8601,	I. Booth,	— — —		20
9 May,	15760,	C. Oliver,	— — —		30
9th Sept	219,	S. D. L. Maziere,	— — —		30
9st June,	11213,	I. Booth,	— — —		20
9th Oct.	14836,	P. Pincan,	— — —		50
9th May,	1002,	T. Donovan,	— — —		50
9th Oct.	12972,	J. Longman,	— — —		40
					50
					50
					540
					£1000

Also, one Kirkby Lonsdale Bank Note for £5 5s. three for £2 2s. each; one of Mr. Wakefield's Kendal
Notes for £5 5s. and two Kendal Bank Notes for £1 1s. each.
*** Whoever will bring the above Notes to Messrs. GORST, solicitors, Preston, or place the same to
their credit, in any of the Banks at Kendal, Lancaster, Preston, Liverpool, or Manchester, shall receive
reward of

FIFTY GUINEAS, on application to Messrs. GORST.

The allied advance across Europe caused immense suffering to the civilian populations, first of Russia and then of Germany. Collections were made in all the churches of the town for their relief and somewhat earlier for British prisoners in France and it is perhaps significant that the amount of money raised by the Society of Friends was second only to that raised by the parish church of St Mary – indicative of the wealth, influence and social position of the Quakers and their relative importance in the trade and industry of the town.[1]

As autumn moved into winter it must have become clear that the end of the war could not be too far off. The winter of 1813/14 was extremely severe, with the mail coaches being delayed on several occasions because of deep snow; and the ice on the canal was too thick to allow the passage of coal barges up to Lancaster. The river Lune itself froze over, thereby allowing a party of four men to skate up to Hornby and back.

To celebrate 'the glorious successes that have recently attended the arms of Great Britain and her allies' a public meeting at the town hall decided that there should be a dinner followed by a ball in the evening to be held at the Assembly Rooms in King Street. This duly took place on 22 December and was clearly a great success, with dancing continuing until four o'clock in the morning. The profits were over £50 and were distributed among local charities, the largest share going to the Dispensary on Castle Hill, which was an out-patients institution for the sick poor. The *Lancaster Gazette* was also able to reassure its readers: 'nor were the lower classes forgotten on this joyous occasion. Many of the tradesmen and manufacturers gave their work people handsome treats at different houses.'

By the early part of the New Year 1814 it was obvious that the end of the war was imminent, with both the British army from Spain and the allied army deep inside the French heartland. Finally, on 7 April news arrived of the surrender of Paris to the Russians, Austrians and Prussians, followed a few days later by the abdication of Napoleon Bonaparte. Jonathan Binns, whose farm lay on the main road immediately south of Lancaster, records the passage of the mail coaches suitably decorated bringing the momentous news,[2] while the *Lancaster Gazette* gave a full report:

> The glorious news which we this week have the pleasure of announcing to our readers of the entry of the Allied Armies into Paris was received here by the Manchester and Liverpool mail [coach] about two o'clock on Thursday morning.

Thus forewarned, many people from the town met

> the London Mail at the end of town [where] it was received with loud huzzas
> and cheered through the principal streets to the Post Office where it was
> greeted with three times three. Numerous parties formed at various houses
> where further success to the Allied Armies were drunk.

The accounts for the Merchants' Newsroom record briefly 'p[ai]d for ribbons
for the Mail Guard and Coachmen on news of the allies in Paris 13s. 4d.',
and shortly after 'Paid do' for News of Peace 10s. od.'[3]

Great celebrations for the arrival of peace took place in Lancaster and the
surrounding district during the second week of July 1814. There was a display
of fireworks on the Green Area near to Skerton Bridge; flags were displayed
on public buildings; and there was an enormous influx of visitors. The public
were warned by a notice from the town clerk, published in the *Lancaster
Gazette*, that good order was essential and that this would be enforced by a
number of special constables as well as the regular 'Peace Officers'. The notice
concluded with a very interesting addendum:

> And, that the peace of the town may not be interrupted it is earnestly
> entreated, that no insult or injury whatsoever be offered to the houses or
> windows of any persons, who, either from religious motives, indisposition of
> their family, absence from home or other reasons, may not choose to illuminate
> their houses on this occasion as the aggressors will answer at their peril.

The 'religious motives' is clearly a reference to the Quakers, whose testimony
against all war was well developed, and suggests a strong degree of tolerance
and respect for dissenters by the members of the town council. All religious
nonconformists, including Roman Catholics, were still prevented by
seventeenth-century legislation from being appointed to the town council.
As part of the celebrations a general illumination of the town took place
and many of the public buildings, principal inns and larger houses displayed
what were called 'transparencies'. These depicted patriotic slogans and pictures
representing ships, commerce, battles and the names of the military and naval
leaders of the allied forces. Illuminated from behind with lamps they were very
popular and the local paper painstakingly described every single one, where
it was displayed and by whom. During the evening the drums and fifes of
the Lonsdale Local Militia 'paraded the town and at different places joined
the populace in repeated cheers.' The final event was a ball 'numerously and
respectably attended'.

> MR EDITOR,
>   IF the account of what passed at our neighbour-
> ing village, of Melling, in commemoration of
> Peace, on Monday last, be worth a place in your
> valuable paper, it will much oblige
>   A CONSTANT READER.
>   On entering this little village, I was much grati-
> fied at seeing two colours flying at the top of the
> steeple, and another handsome one suspended in the
> middle of the town, with the inscription of " Wel-
> lington and Peace ;" the bells rang at intervals the
> whole day, and a band of music paraded the streets.
> Vollies of musketry frequently were fired. In the
> evening, the whole village, amounting to about
> 120, partook of an excellent supper, which was
> announced by a large round of beef and two large
> plumb-puddings carried through the town, upon
> the heads of three tall men, with colours flying and
> the band playing. At each end of the table were
> the bus's of Lord Wellington and General Blucher,
> which had a pretty effect After supper, many ap-
> propriate toasts were drank, God save the King was
> sung in full chorus ; and as much liquor and ale was
> distributed as could be drunk. The villagers spent
> the rest of the evening in dancing, and concluded
> with a handsome illumination. The above was
> under the direction and at the sole expence of Mr.
> Bell, of Melling Hall.
>   On Saturday the 23d ult. Lord Muncaster gave a
> liberal entertainment at the King's-Arms, in Raven-

How the village of Melling celebrated the Peace of 1814.

At the beginning of August another celebration was held at Hornby, whose inhabitants were joined by many others from Melling, Wray, Gressingham and Arkholme. Four hundred pounds of beef, veal and mutton with puddings were provided for the 250 persons present. According to the *Lancaster Gazette*, 'About 100 gallons of ale and grog were the means of putting the assembly in good spirits.' No doubt it did indeed have that effect.

That victory summer of 1814 must have seemed like a dream to many people. After years of struggle, disappointment and hardship the arrival of peace must surely have meant the promise of peace, plenty and international harmony. As part of the latter, there was a visit in the spring and early summer of the allied sovereigns and their military commanders led by the Emperor of Russia, to London. By chance the Reverend Bryan Waller was visiting London from his vicarage at Burton-in-Kendal and while in Hart Street, Bloomsbury, saw 'the Emperor Alexander, the King of Prussia and other illustrious strangers who had paid a visit to this metropolis'.[4]

Sadly, the early hopes of the people were not fulfilled; in fact the next twenty years or so was a period of great social hardship and political turmoil. As 1814 slipped into 1815 the first signs of an economic downturn appeared, with a fall in agricultural prices and the failure in demand for manufactured goods both at home and abroad. As far as Lancaster was concerned, the demand for colonial produce such as sugar, rum and coffee declined also. As for Lancaster shipping, 1814 was the last year ever when the number of ships arriving from the West Indies reached double figures.

The early part of 1815 was also convulsed by events on the international stage, with the escape of Napoleon from the island of Elba, to which he had been exiled by the victorious allies the previous year. Napoleon quickly retook power in Paris, but his final reign proved in the end fortunately, short-lived: at the end of June news of the overwhelming allied victory at the battle of Waterloo was received in Lancaster with the usual rejoicings, although John Higgin, the governor of the castle prison, noted somewhat sourly in his journal for 24 June: 'Much roaring and singing among the debtors in [room] No. 7. The News of the Day being an excuse as they imagine for Intemperance.'[5] However, very much to its credit a town meeting, chaired by the mayor, decided to have a collection throughout the area for the families of those killed and for the wounded. The very large sum of over £700 was collected, with the local paper publishing a list of all the subscribers. Many of the names shown are familiar and have already appeared in the earlier pages of this book, including members of the Worswick banking family, Gillows, Redmayne, West Indian names such as Burrow and Nottage, Moore, Hinde and Salisbury. Brockbanks and Smiths, the two shipbuilders, contributed, as did Fenton Cawthorne and Charles Gibson, together with several of the ships' captains we have encountered, including Thomas Greenwood, John Charnley, Thomas Wilson, Nicholas Carter and others. As the *Lancaster Gazette* so aptly put it:

> It seems right that gentlemen of known fortune and nobleness of mind
> should have their generosity published as a splendid example to others, if any
> stimulus should be wanting on such an occasion.

However, a total of fifty-three women also contributed to the collection, including Mrs Hargreaves from Springfield Hall (the site of which is now occupied by the newest part of the Royal Lancaster Infirmary), three more members of the Hinde family and other 'West Indian' names such as Satterthwaite and Suart. Miss Belasyse, the sister of Lord Fauconberg who lived in Thurnham Street, made a contribution. From Skerton, among others was Mrs Nunns, doubtless the widow of the notorious Captain John Nunns, and finally even the girls in the charity school gave 5s. 2d.

The despatch of the total sum collected to London in September 1815 (and the disbanding of the 1st Royal Lancaster Militia in the following March) really marked the end of the war for Lancastrians. For the bereaved, the wounded and the crippled the legacy was a more lasting one.[6] The end of the war also coincided very clearly with the severe and permanent decline of Lancaster's involvement in the West Indian trade, upon which so much of the prosperity of the town had been founded for the previous half-century. This in turn led to the contraction or disappearance of shipbuilding and its ancillary

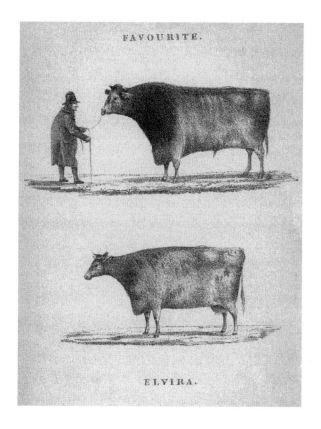

Elvira, a pure-bred Durham shorthorn, was purchased by Jonathan Binns in 1813. He farmed at Leech House almost opposite Lancaster University. She was always served by Favourite and was still alive in 1821 at the age of sixteen years.

FROM THE AGRICULTURE OF LANCASHIRE. REPRODUCED BY PERMISSION OF THE COUNTY ARCHIVIST, LANCASHIRE RECORD OFFICE

trades, including sail and sailcloth making, rope making and anchor making. Only the furniture factory of Gillows and George Crossfield's sugar refining business (situated in Sugar House Alley) were able to survive. Agricultural prices also fell, bringing disaster to many farmers such as Jonathan Binns, who wrote: 'The effect of this glorious peace was the reduction of agricultural produce ruinously to me'. In December 1815 the *Lancaster Gazette* reported:

> Garstang Fair is remarkable for Scotch cattle. It is held in the fields and continues two or three days. The quantity of Scotch cattle is more than at all the fairs in Lancashire in a year; some years there have been upward of 3,000 head; the last year there was about 2,300 and nearly all sold. This year only 1800 and not half sold though at reduced prices; this shows the want of money among the farmers.

This agricultural recession was of course not restricted to north Lancashire it was a countrywide occurrence and led directly to the passing of the famous Corn Laws which restricted the import of cheap foreign corn in an effort to support the powerful home agricultural interest and whose existence bedevilled British politics until their repeal some thirty years later.

The third blow suffered in 1815 was the beginning of a major industrial depression. Ironically this perhaps did not affect Lancaster as much as the loss of the West Indian trade and the decline in farming because there was no big manufacturing concern in the town – at least not in that era. But the collapse in the West Indian trade was a grievous blow not only to Lancaster's prosperity but also to its pride.

Perhaps the most remarkable aspect of Lancaster's time as an important West India port is that it ever happened in the first place. In retrospect its decline and fall were probably inevitable. The reason for this loss must surely be that Lancaster was simply in the wrong place. The superiority of Liverpool as a port was immense, having a better river and having far more local capital to develop the docks and improve the navigation to such an extent that Lancaster could just not compete. In addition there was the vast industrial hinterland of south Lancashire, to which Liverpool was connected by a network of recently constructed canals and waterways. This industrial area demanded enormous imports and produced equally large exports, much of which based on the booming textile industry of the North West. As a port there was never going to be a contest between Lancaster and Liverpool and unfortunately the former had nothing to substitute for its West Indian trade – unlike say Whitehaven, which had prospered on the trans-Atlantic tobacco trade and when that went was able to switch to coal from the nearby West Cumberland coalfield. Lancaster had no such alternative and although the coastal trade through Glasson Dock and the canal still continued, the glory days had clearly gone.[7] Lancaster (like Chester, whose river silted up and whose port and overseas trade collapsed even more completely than that of Lancaster) remained a quiet town run by a network of local gentry and self-elected freemen together with the more affluent of the local shopkeepers and tradesmen. Twice a year the town was enlivened by the arrival of the assizes with their attendant crowd of lawyers, witnesses and hangers-on bringing money and some social life into the place because Lancaster was, until 1834, the only assize town in the whole of the county and attracted the patronage of the cream of Lancashire society. But all this could not ensure Lancaster's prosperity and neither did the attempts by individuals to turn Lancaster into an industrial town really succeed until the rise of the Williamson and Storey dynasties in the second half of the nineteenth century.[8]

Some of the West Indian merchants like the Rawlinsons retired or moved their businesses to Liverpool and among those remaining there was perhaps a lack of spirit and enterprise together with the shortage of capital towards improving the port and river. There has always been a movement away from Lancaster (which has continued to this day) of many of the best qualified and most capable sons and daughters of the city and this really began to be discernible in the early 1800s. Perhaps old Lancaster really died with the collapse of the two private banks, both founded on the transatlantic trade – Worswicks in 1822 and Dilworth and Co. four years later, bringing ruin to many and hardship to all. By the time the railways arrived in 1840 the world, and Lancaster's place within it had changed completely. For more than half a century Lancaster had been an outward-looking maritime centre with connections and interests far overseas. The wealth brought by trade and the local industries which had grown up to service it had led to the construction of a fine if incomplete Georgian provincial town, with elegant town houses, warehouses and public buildings, many of which adorn the streets today.

And what remains today of the glory days of the port of Lancaster? The beautiful eighteenth-century Customs House retains its pride of place on the river's edge, fortunately still unspoilt and unencumbered by later development. Liverpool might have become the most important port city in the country, but its ancient Customs Houses have been lost. The warehouses which line St George's Quay are also largely unchanged, except in how they are used, and late twentieth-century development alongside has even sought to emulate their design and scale in order to retain the character of the river frontage. The only truly modern office block has been built on the northern bank of the river near to the site of Smith's old shipyard.

Because Lancaster's maritime trade fell away so precipitously, and because Lancaster did not develop a large industrial sector there was to be no grandiose dock scheme as at Preston. However, the Williamson complex on St George's Quay was partly serviced by coasters bringing china clay from Cornwall and other raw materials well into the second half of the twentieth century. Otherwise the railway and canal provided transport for local industry until road transport took over after the Second World War.

Apart from the quay at Lancaster there is of course Glasson Dock itself. With the dock facilities improved in the last twenty years it now possesses a thriving marina and it is still used commercially by coasting vessels and the occasional foreign ship. Pier Hall, once the resort of the ships' crews on their return from overseas, became the Caribou Hotel and has recently been converted into flats. Otherwise the layout of the dock remains much the same as when it played host to the *Aurora*, the *Paragon*, the *Neptune* and the *Mars* and all those other ships of long ago with their captains and their crews from Lancaster who braved the elements and who sometimes fought off and who were sometimes taken by the enemies of their country during the period of time covered by the last and greatest war with France. As we have seen, in that titanic struggle Lancaster and its people in their various ways had played their part.

APPENDIX A

Population of Lancaster and district

	1801	*1811*
Lancaster	9,030	9,247
Skerton	1,278	1,254
Bulk	100	113
Scotforth	462	466
Total	10,870	12,070

Lancaster ships

IT IS NOT ALWAYS EASY TO DEFINE a Lancaster ship. Five possible definitions seem to arise, as follows:

1. Built in Lancaster at either Brockbanks' or Smiths' Yard
2. Registered in Lancaster
3. Owned or partly owned by Lancastrians
4. Sailing regularly to and from Lancaster or Glasson
5. Crewed by Lancastrians.

In the two lists that follow all the vessels fall into one of the above categories and some more than one. Most (but not all) of the Lancaster-built ships appear to have been registered, initially at least, at Lancaster. As the wars progressed there was a tendency for the ships to be owned by a mixed consortium of Lancaster and Liverpool people. Throughout the period a resident in one of the West Indian islands is also very frequently shown as having an interest in a ship, as is the ship's captain. It is clear from the Lancaster Ships Registers that ships are frequently transferred by Lancaster owners to Liverpool (and other) owners in line with the shifting balance of the overseas shipping trade to the Mersey. Some ship owners also transferred their business to Liverpool. It is also worthy of note that both Brockbanks and Smiths built for non-Lancaster owners in Liverpool, London and Glasgow, though these were not usually registered in Lancaster. However, the bulk of the construction in both yards was for Lancaster. Both Brockbanks and Smiths also built plenty of quite small craft, including fishing boats, canal boats and coasters, and seem also to have carried out basic joinery work for individual customers.

All the ships whose names now follow appear to have had a substantial connection with Lancaster and fall into one of the first four categories listed above – particularly the first. Present knowledge is insufficient to list those ships crewed mainly by Lancastrians. In any event it seems likely that the crews sailed without discrimination from either Liverpool or Lancaster (and elsewhere) and took ship whenever there was a vacant berth and that ships sailed to and from either port (and also elsewhere) depending on available cargo or market. Sometimes ships bound for the West Indies cleared from Liverpool before sailing round to Lancaster and vice versa. Most sailed in convoy which they joined at Cork.

Brockbanks' last seagoing ship (the *Thomas and Nancy*) was built in 1817. Their yard seems to have closed in about 1820, spending the last three years engaged in either repairs or building canal boats. The Smiths left Lancaster for Liverpool in 1816 (their last local ship, the *Active*, was launched in August of that year), where they remained in business as shipbuilders until 1867. Their yard in Skerton was sold and continued to produce ships until 1827, albeit on a reduced scale. Both firms were obviously very seriously affected by the collapse in the Lancaster West Indian trade after the end of the war in 1815.

Neither of the following lists claims to be totally accurate or complete. The re-use of names often makes proper identification difficult. It is clear, however, that, whatever the causes, the losses to a small place like Lancaster were substantial.

In view of the excellent reputation acquired by John Brockbank as a shipbuilder it is perhaps surprising that his firm did not (so far as it is known) build any ships for the Royal Navy which was a huge organisation. In 1810 it comprised 152 ships of the line (64 guns or more) and 183 cruisers such as frigates. These ships were probably too big for the facilities at the Brockbank shipyard, but the Navy would have required many smaller craft which could have been built locally. Interestingly enough the *Lancaster Gazette* reported in September 1805 that Admiral Earl St Vincent (a former First Lord of the Admiralty) and Admiral Troubridge visited Lancaster, staying overnight at the King's Arms Hotel. Next morning they toured Lancaster and then visited Brockbank's shipyard. Common sense suggests that when two of the leading and most distinguished naval figures of the day met John Brockbank the question of doing work for the Navy must have arisen during conversation. However, nothing came of it and one can only assume that Brockbank was happy with his current position and did not need to do work for what could possibly be a difficult and demanding client.

Ships taken or sunk by the enemy, 1793–1815

Name of Ship	Name of Captain	Remarks
Watson	Richard Nicholson	Taken 1794
Apollo	Thomas Strickland	Taken 1794
William	John Graham	Taken 1794
Liberty	William Hart	Sunk 1794
The Molly		Taken 1794

Name of Ship	Name of Captain	Remarks
Reynolds	William Neale	Taken 1795
Britannia	Thomas Roper	Taken 1796
Henry	Henry Parker	Taken 1796
The Vine (1)	William Greaves	Taken 1796
Best	William Croft	Taken 1796
Friends	Peter Jackson	Taken 1797
Chatsworth	Henry Lawson	Taken 1797
Diana	William Bayne	Taken 1797
William	–	Taken 1797
Ann	John Roper	Taken 1797
Mary	James Medcalfe	Taken and retaken 1797/98
Dolphin	Dennis Murphy	Taken 1797
Alexander	John Pawson	Taken 1797
Hope	Thomas Atkinson	Taken 1797
Maxwell	–	Taken and re-taken 1798
Union	Thomas Caton	Taken 1798
Granville Bay	George Gray	Taken and re-taken 1799
Lydia	William Kellet	Taken 1799
Union	William Thompson	Taken 1799
Hygeia	John Pawson	Taken 1799
Brothers	Leonard Redmayne	Taken 1799
Argo	Thomas Kidd	Taken 1799
Fairy	Alexander Foster	Taken 1799
Venerable	John Croft	Taken and re-taken 1802
Speculation	Richard Winder	Taken 1799
George	– Lowther	Taken 1799
Sally	James Derbyshire	Taken 1800
Richard	William Thompson	Taken 1801
Activa	William McDowell	Taken 1800
Robert	Jonathan Derbyshire	Taken and re-taken
Europa (1)	–	Taken 1798
Valentine	George Nicholson	Taken 1807
Fortitude	Robert Frears	Taken and re-taken 1807
Harriet	Davis Thompson	Taken and re-taken 1807
Pitt	Captain Campbell	Taken 1807
Thomas	William Thompson	Taken and re-taken 1807
Neptune	Thomas Wilson	Taken and re-taken 1809
Eliza	George Taylor	Taken 1812
John of Gaunt	Peter Inglis	Taken and burnt 1813
John	Captain Campbell	Taken 1812

Name of Ship	Name of Captain	Remarks
The Brothers	John Bragg	Taken 1813
Neptune	Thomas Dawson	Taken and released 1814

N.B. (1) The last three vessels were taken by American ships during the war of 1812–15, including the second taking of the *Neptune*.

(2) At least four or five ships registered at Lancaster but stated to be 'of Ulverston' were also taken in the early part of the war. Probable names – *Ellen* (two ships), *Tom, Reynolds* and *Albion*.

(3) In the war of 1776–83, twenty-five ships belonging to Lancaster were taken by the enemy and thirteen lost due to the natural perils of the sea.

Ships lost, foundered or wrecked, 1793–1815

Name of Ship	Name of Captain	Remarks
Cohen	Joseph Davies	Lost 1793
Betty and Sally	John Hordiker	Lost 1794
Rawlinson	George Warbrick	Lost 1794
Clypea		Lost 1797
Aurora (1)	John Robinson	Lost 1799
Albion	John Tatterson (?)	
Mildred	Thomas Atkinson	Lost 1800
Scipio	John Croft	Lost 1800
Lancaster	Thomas Wilson	Lost 1802
Langton	William Kellet	Lost 1803
Europa (2)	William Bradley	Lost 1802
Britannia	Robert Taylor	Lost 1802
Endevour	–	Lost 1804
Demerara	Peter Inglis	Lost 1804
Harriet	Davis Thompson	Lost 1808
Tyson	John Pawson	Lost 1805
Myrtle	Thomas Harper	Lost 1808
Arrow	James Taylor	Lost 1805
Sally	Thomas Potter	Lost 1809
Grenada	Thomas Oxton	Lost 1810
Adventure	– McMillen	Lost 1810
Nancy	– McMillen	Lost 1812
The Unity	– Hardy	Lost 1814
Laurel	– Emmett	Lost 1815

Lancaster Overseas Trade, 1793–1816

1. Ships from the West Indies

1793	39	1801	20	1809	20
1794	34	1802	8	1810	18
1795	40	1803	12	1811	18
1796	40	1804	12	1812	9
1797	39	1805	14	1813	15
1798	47	1806	14	1814	13
1799	57	1807	18	1815	3
1800	43	1808	18	1816	3

2. The African (Slave) Trade

One ship yearly from 1785 until 1807 after which, the trade having become illegal, no further figure given. The figure for Liverpool is usually over one hundred per year. The Lancaster involvement in the Slave Trade was highest during the 1760s, when on average five ships were employed yearly. After 1799 by law any Lancaster slave ships would have to clear via Liverpool. However, Lancaster's involvement in the African Trade was larger than appears from the number of ships employed due to Lancaster merchants like the Hinde family increasingly operating solely from Liverpool or investing in slaving ventures from that port. The Act of Parliament abolishing the Slave Trade came into force on 1st May, 1807. It seems, however, that if a slave ship was fitting out at that time the 'cut off' date could be extended. The very last British slave ship appears to have been the Liverpool registered *Eliza* (Captain Samuel Hensley), which cleared that port on the 16th August, 1807, bound for Old Calabar in West Africa.

Despite the small size of the Lancaster share in the Slave Trade (as compared to the other ports of Liverpool, London and Bristol) it is abundantly clear that the town and its inhabitants benefited hugely from the trade with the West Indies. Exporting manufactured items and importing high value goods consisting of sugar, rum, cotton, coffee, mahogany and other timbers. Some of the plantations in the West Indies and the slaves who worked them also belonged to Lancaster citizens.

The abolition of slavery in the British Empire in 1834 was only accomplished on the payment by the British Government of very large sums of money to the owners of the slaves some of whom were Lancastrians. That there was any compensation at all was due to the sacred concept of property which, however repellent to us today, was applied, not only to land, goods and chattels, but also to human beings.

The fact that a high proportion of the compensation monies was subsequently invested in sections of the burgeoning industrial revolution – particularly the railways, does not make it any more palatable today.

3. Remaining Trade

This consisted of ships from the Baltic, Hamburg, Oporto and North America. In addition there was a very substantial coastal trade on the West coast of Britain together with voyages to Ireland and the Isle of Man. The total figures for all shipping, including those in (1) and (2) above, are as follows:

1793	257	1801	224	1809	214
1794	253	1802	225	1810	263
1795	283	1803	239	1811	170
1796	284	1804	221	1812	171
1797	269	1805	236	1813	201
1798	339	1806	258	1814	187
1799	345	1807	210	1815	213
1800	330	1808	192	1816	244

Until the coming of the railways most heavy and bulky materials had to be carried by coastal and canal shipping.

Letters of marque

These would be issued (on application) to ships allowing them to seek and capture merchant ships of hostile countries, which in our period were mainly French, Spanish, Dutch, Danish and some Italian. The captured ships and cargoes would then be sold and the proceeds retained.

The number of letters of marque issued for Lancaster are as follows with figures for Liverpool shown to emphasise the difference in scale between the two ports. However, although a long way behind, Lancaster was fifth during each phase of the war.

| 1793–1801 | Lancaster | 62 | Liverpool | 1691 |
| 1803–1815 | Lancaster | 33 | Liverpool | 1267 |

Source: David Starkey, *British Privateering Enterprise in the Eighteenth Century* (1990).

Notes and references

Note to Introduction

1. Quoted in C. Emsley, *British Society and the French Wars* (1979).

Notes to Chapter 1: Setting the scene

1. Summarized in Clark, *History of Lancaster* (1807), pp. 119–21. See Appendix A for a breakdown of the population figures.
2. Lancashire Record Office, DDX 760/1, Cragg Diary.
3. Brockbanks' employees in December 1795 and November 1811 were as follows:

1795	1811
36 shipwrights	33 shipwrights
20 apprentices	29 apprentices
8 pairs of sawyers (i.e. 16 persons)	10 pairs of sawyers (i.e. 20 persons)
12 labourers	13 labourers
8 joiners	9 joiners
8 carters, painters and trenellers	plus 1 clerk

Source: Lancaster City Reference Library, MS 241/242/3721, Brockbank papers.

4. The *Lancaster Gazette* published details of membership each year in May.

Notes to Chapter 2: The other half

1. Page 68.
2. See various directories, 1794–1825.
3. Lancaster City Reference Library.
4. Membership of a Friendly Society gave some protection from the harsher provisions of the Poor Law.
5. Lancaster City Reference Library, MSS 1627 and 1658.
6. Lancaster City Reference Library, MS 6041.
7. *Lancaster Gazette*, 16th July, 1811. In October 1809 Alice Morland was sentenced to six months' imprisonment for stealing a pair of sheets from the King's Arms Hotel.

8. The columns of the *Lancaster Gazette* are full of such occurrences. In December 1805 the same paper gave details of a wife being 'sold' by her husband at Horse Shoe Corner.
9. An example appears in the *Lancaster Gazette* of 8th January 1814.

Notes to Chapter 3: The parson and the farmer

1. Lancashire Record Office, DDX 3/114, Waller Journal.
2. Some original correspondence is at Lancaster City Reference Library, MSS 5735–5737.
3. The writer met her once, briefly, as a small boy.
4. Cragg Diary. See notes on sources.
5. See Minutes of the Amicable Library at Lancaster City Reference Library, MS 211.

Notes to Chapter 4: The seamen

1. See Appendix B.
2. The total merchant shipping losses for the war were probably about 8500 vessels. However, according to the Secretary of Lloyds this amounted to only 2% yearly which in economic terms was bearable (Woodward, p. 559).
3. Lancaster City Reference Library, MS 1668.
4. For information relating to Lancaster ships and ships' masters and their adventures prior to 1801 see (a) Hewetson's *Memoranda*, vol. 1 (extracts from Manchester Mercury), (b) Copied extracts from Liverpool and Whitehaven newspapers at Lancaster City Reference Library, PT 8366, 8367, 8365, 8368, (c) Register of Lancaster Shipping, Lancashire County Record Office, SS/5/1, (d) Copy Seamen's Sixpence Register, Lancaster City Reference Library, PT 8822, (e) After 1801 the *Lancaster Gazette* provides an additional invaluable though spasmodic source. It is on film at the Lancaster City Reference Library. (f) Brockbank records at Lancaster City Reference Library MS 421/242/3721, (g) Financial details and letter books of A. and J. Rawlinson, Lancaster City Reference Library, MSS 3715, 3719 and 239.
5. See Appendix B.
6. The *Clorinde* was subsequently intercepted by the Royal Navy frigate *Eurotas*. After a desperate struggle she was taken and carried into Portsmouth.

Notes to Chapter 5: The sea captains

1. Will at Lancashire Record Office, WRW/A R163a.
2. Liverpool Shipping Registers (at Liverpool Maritime Museum).
3. The National Archives, Series ADM 103.
4. Will at Lancashire Record Office, WRW/A, R140.
5. Details of burials were recorded before gravestones removed c. 1970.
6. T.C. Hughes. Article Lancashire and Cheshire Antiquarian Society, vol. XXXIV, 1916, p 220.
7. The Hinde family appear to have been inveterate Slave Traders to the bitter end. Two of Samuel Hinde's children were still alive in the early 1900s – one, a son, in Bournmouth and Miss Mabella Hinde in South Place, Lancaster, now the upper part of Dallas Road.
8. Mr Walmsley's brother served in the Royal Navy and was present at the battle of Camperdown.

9. There is a memorial to the young dragoon officer in Lancaster Priory Church.
10. Captain Carter and his crew were suitably rewarded by the insurance underwriters.
11. Will at Lancashire Record Office, WRW/R125a/26.

Notes to Chapter 6: The last voyage of Captain Thomas Greenwood

1. See Scrapbook 2(2) at Lancaster City Reference Library. Two of Thomas Greenwood's sons were still living in Lancaster during the 1880s and no doubt were the owners of the manuscript and made it available to Hewitson.
2. Other members of the family were surgeons and furniture makers. Isaac was a favourite name in the family. This particular Isaac was quite wealthy when he died in 1839 owning a lot of rented-out house property in Lancaster.
3. The press cutting relating to the second voyage of the *Mars* is missing from the Scrapbook.
4. Seamen's Sixpence Register, Lancaster City Reference Library, PT 8822.
5. *Pusey Hall.* This was the second Lancaster ship of that name and was called after the Pusey Hall plantation situated in the parish of Vere on the island of Jamaica. The Harrison family of Springfield Hall, Lancaster, seem to have been the owners or part-owners of the plantation. Pusey Hall sugars were imported into Lancaster for many years. The ship carried 14 nine-pounder guns, a sufficient armament to allow her to sail independently of the otherwise obligatory convoy.
6. See letter book of James Moore & Co., Lancashire County Record Office, DP 409/1. Through the marriage of their niece the partners in the firm became the great-great-uncles of Beatrix Potter of 'Peter Rabbit' fame. Her mother was brought up at Lune Villa in Skerton, which was then occupied by the Crompton family, well known Unitarians.
7. Lancaster City Reference Library, MS 5084.
8. The engagement took place approximately 800–900 miles west off Land's End.
9. Will at Lancashire Record Office, WRW/R162/64.

Notes to Chapter 7: Manning the Royal Navy

1. Lancaster City Reference Library, MS 5169. In the summer of 1806 the coastal vessel *Dundee* en route from Peterhead to Lancaster was detained by a Royal Naval frigate and had eighteen members of her crew pressed forthwith.
2. Lewis' *Social History of the Navy.*
3. Lancashire Record Office, QDV/1 and QDV/26.
4. *A Naval Biographical Dictionary*, W. O'Byrne, 1847.
5. *Lancaster and District Seamen at Trafalgar*, R. White, Lancaster, 2005. Lambert went on to have a quite exciting naval career rising to the rank of Lieutenant, being wounded twice and being temporarily captured by both the French and the Americans.
6. Lancaster City Reference Library, pp 404–7.
7. For crew muster lists see National Archives, Series ADM 36 and 37. There is a graphic account of the wreck of the *Anson* in *The War for all the Oceans* by Adkins (Little Brown, 2006).
8. Ladies' Walk was an attractive tree-lined walkway on the south side of the River Lune extending upstream from Skerton Bridge for about a mile. Built over with roads and railway sidings in the First World War.

Notes to Chapter 8: The soldiers

1. Hall. *British Strategy.*
2. See Lancashire Record Office, Quarter Sessions Petitions (QSP), throughout the period.
3. The original Minutes relating to the Loyal Lancaster Volunteers are held at Lancashire County Record Office (DDQ 28/2) and cover the period 1797–1802 only.
4. Bryant. *Years of Victory*, p 1.
5. Most of the information regarding the post-1803 Volunteers, the local militia and the county militia has been obtained from the *Lancaster Gazette* over the years 1803–1814.
6. 'It was no fault of theirs (the Prime Minister, Addington, and the Secretary for War, Lord Hobart) that England was not ruined both in a financial and military sense so unspeakable was their blindness, their weakness and their folly.' Fortescue, *The County Lieutenancies and the Army*, 1914, p 283. However, in December 1803 the total number of volunteers reached 400,000.
7. Series WO 97 and WO 121 at the National Archives, Kew. Casualties are in Series WO 25, arranged under regiments. For British prisoners in France see Series ADM 103–105. A number of both seamen and soldiers from Lancaster have been identified as confined in various French fortresses, like Sarrelibre, Arras and Givet. In 1806 there were four seamen from Ulverston as prisoners at Valenciennes.

Notes to Chapter 9: The politician, the gentleman and the absentee vicar

1. For Cawthorne see Cragg, *Lancaster Gazette*, election literature (examples at Lancaster City Reference Library) and *Lonsdale Magazine*, vol. II, 1821, and *The House of Commons 1790–1820* edited by R.G. Thorne, 1985.
2. For White see Hewetson, information from Clare College, Cambridge, and information and copy correspondence supplied by present members of the family in London.
3. For Gibson see Binns MSS (Lancaster City Reference Library), Garnett papers (Lancashire County Record Office), Minutes of Loyal Lancaster Volunteers, *Lancaster Gazette* and information supplied by his descendants in New Zealand.

Notes to Chapter 10: Hardship and tragedy

1. See J.D. Marshall, *Old Lakeland*, Chapter 5.
2. Lancashire Record Office, Quarter Sessions Petitions for those years.
3. Colley, p 332.
4. Lancaster City Reference Library, MS 2466.

Notes to Chapter 11: The bitterness of victory and the end of old Lancaster

1. Figures for the prisoner collection were as follows:
      Parish Church of St Mary's: £61
      Society of Friends (Quakers): £52
      St John's: £31
      St Ann's: £19
      Catholic Chapel: £15.
      For the distressed Germans:

Parish Church of St Mary's: £86

Society of Friends (Quakers): £185

Lancaster Gazette, 12th March 1814.

2. Lancaster City Reference Library, Binns MSS 7054–7056.

3. Merchants' News Room Accounts held by the Lancaster Chamber of Commerce.

4. Waller Journal.

5. John Higgin Journal, Lancaster City Reference Library.

6. Like Lieutenant Thomas Satterthwaite of Carnforth who died in July 1815 'of excessive fatigue and hard service on the coast of America during the late war', and William Buckley of the Commissariat Department wo died at Plymouth in June 1814 'through a disorder brought on by excessive fatigue in Spain'.

7. Other possible factors in the decline of the West India trade were the uneconomic characteristics of a slave-based economy, the loss of much of the seaborne carrying trade from the West Indies which was undercut by American shipping during the period up to 1812 and which seems to have used Liverpool as their British entry port and later the replacement of the West Indies by the southern States of the USA as the main raw cotton-producing area. In July 1809 there were over 100 American ships available for charter at Liverpool. The matter is discussed in depth in Schofield, Chapters 7 and 8.

8. The amount paid in Poor Rate by way of relief rose gradually from 1809 onwards with a major jump of over thirty per cent for the twelve months ended at Easter 1817. MS 1694, Lancaster City Reference Library.

Further reading

General

Although now obviously outdated by more recent research and scholarship, Sir Arthur Bryant's trilogy, *The Years of Endurance*, *The Years of Victory* and *The Age of Elegance*, published between 1941 and 1950, provides a very good and highly readable overview of the period from 1793 to 1822, notwithstanding the somewhat rose-tinted spectacles he dons from time to time. A more recent, though much shorter, study is in the later chapters of *Albion Ascendant* by Wilfred Prest (Oxford, 1998), which is very helpful on the political, social, economic and religious factors that were so important in this period. A different view of society is powerfully depicted in E. P. Thompson's *Making of the English Working Class* (Pelican, 1968), although his conclusions have not always received general acceptance. For an account of the forging of a British national identity during the wars, *Britons* by Linda Colley (Vintage, 1996), is essential reading. Also, Roger Knight's *Britain Against Napoleon The Organization of Victory 1793-1815* (Allen Lane 2013) is not a military history but an excellent account of the administrative, financial and organisational problems which were overcome to make victory possible. Finally, Jenny Uglow's *In these Times* (Faber and Faber 2014) is not a military history either but describes very well how the long war years greatly affected the civilian population who were not actively involved in combat on land or sea.

For naval matters the later chapters of *The Command of the Ocean* by N. A. M. Rodger (Allen Lane, 2004) are very helpful; this is a tremendous book by any standard. *A Social History of the Navy, 1793–1815* by Michael Lewis (reprinted by Chatham, 2004) is also excellent, as is the same writer's *Napoleon and His British Captives* (Allen & Unwin, 1962). For the army there is Philip Haythornthwaite's *The Armies of Wellington* (Arms & Armour, 1994). For Lancashire's part in the Luddite disturbances of 1812, these are well described in Robert Reid's *Land of Lost Content* (Heinemann, 1986). For background, very useful are C. Emsley's *British Society and the French Wars* (1979) and Hall's *British Strategy in the Napoleonic War, 1803–1815* (Manchester University Press, 1992).

For information on the enormous scale and importance of the cattle droving industry *The Drovers* by KJ Bonser Macmillan and Co Ltd 1970 seems to be the only major source.

Local

The starting point has to be *A History of Lancaster*, edited by Andrew White (2nd edn, Edinburgh University Press, 2001), particularly chapter 4 (by Nigel Dalziel) and chapter 5 (by Michael Winstanley). Also very helpful is Andrew White's own *Lancaster: A History* (Phillimore, 2003) and *Life in Georgian Lancaster* (Carnegie, 2004). Clark's *History of Lancaster*, published in 1807, has useful information as to matters current at that time. Cross Fleury's monumental *Time Honoured Lancaster* (1891) contains little that is helpful and contains no information as to sources; it is also very badly written. Interestingly it is almost entirely silent on the West Indian and particularly the Slave Trade. This is a pity because at the very least he must have had interesting anecdotal information about both. Quite the opposite is Part 2 of *Outlines of an Economic History of Lancaster, 1680–1860* by the late Maurice Schofield and published by the Lancaster branch of the Historical Association in 1951, now long out of print; it is full of vital information and is essential reading, particularly for the late eighteenth and early nineteenth centuries. See also his *Slave Trade from Lancashire and Cheshire Ports outside Liverpool*, published by the Historic Society of Lancashire and Cheshire (1977). *The Slave Trade and the Economic Development of Eighteenth-century Lancaster* by M. Elder is self-explanatory and provides an excellent and in-depth study of the 'Africa Trade', particularly during its early and middle periods, when it was at its height; it also contains useful information on the activities of the notorious Hinde family. For a general history of the slave trade, see *The Slave Trade* by Hugh Thomas (Picador, 1997). The first half of *The West Indies and the Arctic in the age of sail – the voyages of the Abram (1806–62)*, by Rob David and Michael Winstanley and published by the Centre for NW Regional Studies (2013) gives much invaluable information on the later stages of the Lancaster West Indies trade.

Newspapers

The *Lancaster Gazette* (originally the *Lancaster Gazetteer*) was first published in June 1801. It is an invaluable source of local history and is available on film at the Lancaster City Reference Library. The original is far more useful than the excerpts published in 1869 under the title *Lancaster Records or Leaves from Local History*, although the latter can be helpful. Linda Moorhouse has made great use of the originals in her *Gude Old Town of Lancaster* for the year 1803 and for details of the peace celebrations in 1814. For a period prior to 1801 there are type-written extracts from the *Cumberland Pacquet* and Gore's *Liverpool Advertiser*, relating to Lancaster shipping, in the Lancaster City Reference Library; these were prepared around 1946/47 by S. Rees and are very informative. Information for the same period from the *Manchester Mercury* was included by W. Hewetson in his *Memoranda* (late nineteenth century, two volumes at the Lancaster City Reference Library).

Diaries and Journals

Extensive use has been made of both the Cragg and Waller diaries or journals. Hand-written copies of both of these are in the Lancashire Record Office, Bow Lane, Preston, and they do require some clarification. In 1974 a book entitled *The Craggs of Greenbank*, by Georgina Fandrey (née Cragg) was published privately in Canada. The earlier part of this is based almost entirely on records left by David Cragg (Mrs Fandrey's great-grandfather) which he seems to have taken to Canada when he emigrated in 1833. The original documents are clearly still in Canada, though Mrs Fandrey (now deceased) does not say where; hopefully they are in safe hands. The copy diary at Preston is only part of the Cragg records and was made possibly some time in the mid- or later nineteenth century, by an unidentified person. Much of the information extracted by Mrs Fandrey for *The Craggs of Greenbank* is purely personal and relates to family matters only, while the Preston document gives much more information on public and local affairs and events and the diarist's involvement in them. There is no reason to doubt the accuracy of either and much of the information can be cross-checked with other sources.

Since the above was written the Cragg records have been transcribed (with commentary) by Katrina Navickas in Volume 142 of the Record Society of Lancashire and Cheshire 2006, 'The Cragg Family of Wyresdale'.

The journal of Revd Bryan Waller at the Lancashire Record Office is also a copy. It was transcribed, probably in the late 1950s, by the late Mrs Amy Hallam of Lancaster. This lady was known to me and was, I suspect, a friend of Miss Eleanor Waller, the last of the family who died in 1954. The whereabouts of the original are not known (it is not at the Cumbria Record Office), but again there seems little reason to doubt the accuracy of the copy as some of the contents can be verified by other sources.

Index